What others are saying about

Igniting *Passion* in Your Church

"Every time I'm around Steve Ayers, I am reminded what 'high octane' really means! His is a story of a radical approach in a traditional context that has resulted in an amazing biblical community."

—*Erwin Raphael McManus*, Lead Pastor, Mosaic, Los Angeles, California

"If America is going to enjoy the same revival that much of the rest of the world is experiencing, local churches have to lead the way by becoming storehouses of life-giving relationships. Steve Ayers reminds us that the place to begin is with our own romance with Jesus and our recognition that we, as a church, are his bride."

—*Ted Haggard*, Senior Pastor, New Life Church, Colorado Springs, Colorado

"*Igniting Passion in Your Church* contains insights from a man of God on fire for the relevance of the church in today's world. Steve Ayers' passion is seen every day in his living and giving, in his coming and going, in his implementation and visioning. As a Christian college president, I have great admiration for a pastor who lives and breathes leadership, Christ-style, in all he does. This book will inspire all who read it to live and minister with a new level of passion and commitment."

—*William H. Crouch, Jr.*, President, Georgetown College, Georgetown, Kentucky

"Here's help for churches who want to radiate the love of Christ
  • by attracting people to Christ and not by spending so much time trying to gain the attention of the world.
  • by throwing down people's ideas of church and embracing Jesus' idea of the church as a bride.
  • and by redefining success. It's not focusing on how big the church is; it's by focusing everything on the big question: Do people love Jesus more as a result of hanging around your church?"

—*Dr. Larry L. Sherman*, Director of Church Planting and Associate Superintendent of the Great Lakes Conference of Evangelical Covenant Churches

Flagship church resources

from Group Publishing

Innovations From Leading Churches

Flagship Church Resources are your shortcut to innovative and effective leadership ideas. You'll find ideas for every area of church leadership, including pastoral ministry, adult ministry, youth ministry, and children's ministry.

Flagship Church Resources are created by the leaders of thriving, dynamic, and trend-setting churches around the country. These nationally recognized teaching churches host regional leadership conferences and are respected by other pastors and church leaders because their approaches to ministry are so effective. These flagship church resources reveal the proven ideas, programs, and principles that these churches have put into practice.

Flagship Church Resources currently available:

- *60 Simple Secrets Every Pastor Should Know*
- *The Perfectly Imperfect Church: Redefining the "Ideal Church"*
- *The Winning Spirit: Empowering Teenagers Through God's Grace*
- *Ultimate Skits: 20 Parables for Driving Home Your Point*
- *Doing Life With God: Real Stories Written by Students*
- *Doing Life With God 2: Real Stories Written by Students*
- *The Visual Edge: Compelling Video Connectors for Your Worship Experience*
- *Mission-Driven Worship: Helping Your Changing Church Celebrate God*
- *An Unstoppable Force: Daring to Become the Church God Had in Mind*
- *A Follower's Life: 12 Group Studies On What It Means to Walk With Jesus*

- *Leadership Essentials for Children's Ministry*
- *Keeping Your Head Above Water: Refreshing Insights for Church Leadership*
- *Seeing Beyond Church Walls: Action Plans for Touching Your Community*
- *unLearning Church: Just When You Thought You Had Leadership All Figured Out!*
- *Morph!: The Texture of Leadership for Tomorrow's Church*
- *The Quest for Christ: Discipling Today's Young Adults*
- *LeadingIdeas: To-the-Point Training for Christian Leaders*
- *Igniting Passion in Your Church: Becoming Intimate With Christ*
- *No More Lone Rangers: How to Build a Team-Centered Youth Ministry*

With more to follow!

Igniting *Passion*
in Your Church

Becoming Intimate With Christ

by

Steve Ayers

Flagship church resources
from Group Publishing

Credits
Creative Development Editor: Paul Woods
Editors: John J. Fanella and Candace McMahan
Chief Creative Officer: Joani Schultz
Assistant Editor: Alison Imbriaco
Art Director: Randy Kady
Interior Designer: Liz Howe
Print Production Artist: Spearhead Worldwide, Inc.
Cover Art Director: Jeff A. Storm
Cover Designer: Alan Furst, Inc.
Production Manager: Peggy Naylor

Library of Congress Cataloging-in-Publication Data
   Ayers, Stephen L., 1964-
     Igniting passion in your church : becoming intimate with Christ / by Stephen L. Ayers.
      p. cm.
   Includes bibliographical references.
     ISBN 0-7644-2451-3 (alk. paper)
   1.   Church. 2. Church renewal. 3. Church-Biblical teaching. I.
Title.
   BV600.3 A94 2002
   262'.7--dc21   2002014068

10 9 8 7 6 5 4 3 2 1   12 11 10 09 08 07 06 05 04 03

Printed in the United States of America.

Contents

12/18

104578

Acknowledgments and Dedication

This book stems from my own struggles, victories, and failures as I've sought to know God and experience the power of the Holy Spirit. I thank Jesus Christ for opening his heart and accepting all of us into the kingdom he has prepared for us.

I thank God for the people of Hillvue Heights Church, who have allowed me to wrestle, explore, struggle in grace, find victory, experience failure, and know passion. I thank them for allowing me to be free to be who I am.

I thank God for my wife, Elizabeth, who has diligently encouraged and pastored me. She has made sure that every word of this book has come from my heart and communicates Jesus' passion for all of us.

I thank our assistant, Amy Willis, who has spent countless hours ensuring that this passion is evident on every page.

I thank Group Publishing and its staff for taking risks, encouraging next-generation pastors, and inviting them to have a place at the table.

I also thank God for pastors, especially the unsung ones. They pastor their churches without fanfare, working in inner cities and in remote, rural areas. I thank God that the body of Christ is everywhere.

I dedicate this book to two very special people: my mother, Kathryn Ayers, and my father, Reginald Ayers. They adopted me as a baby and raised me to be a man of God. I thank God for a mother who prayed for me and loved me as Jesus himself loves me and for a father who demonstrates integrity and character in everything he does. I pray that in some small way this book will honor the one they love the most, our Lord Jesus Christ.

I pray that all of us will understand that Jesus Christ loves us so much that he wants to be married to us.

Living in the marriage,
Steve Ayers

Foreword

Recently I checked into a hotel late at night and was given a key to my room. The elevator was at the far end of the hotel, but I waved off the bellman and hurried to my room, bags in tow.

The elevator door closed, but I couldn't get the elevator to work. It would take me to every floor except the one my room was on. Nothing I did would get me to my assigned floor. After many attempts, I gave up and wearily lugged my things back to the registration desk. I told the attendant that something was wrong with the elevator. It wouldn't go to my floor.

She smiled and told me to use the key I had already been given. All I had to do was insert my key in the slot in the elevator panel. I already possessed the key that would open the doorway to my floor. I just didn't know it or know how to use it.

Steve Ayers has not written another "how to play church" book. He has written a powerful reminder to the church that we already have the keys that we need to unlock the energies of the Spirit in our churches. That key is Christ. Our problem is that we have forgotten that we have that key to the kingdom, and we need help in using what we already have.

A moment of full disclosure. I was Steve's faculty advisor for his doctorate of ministry degree at Drew University. When he first broached the idea of rediscovering this most basic biblical image of the church as the bride of Christ, I discouraged him. "There are at least ninety-six images of the church in the New Testament," I told him. "Pick any one of them, but not this one. This is the least likely to connect with the emerging culture."

I'm glad he didn't listen to me. He pursued his study of the bride metaphor, and in this book he challenges the church to decide which it will be: a bride or a business. If a business, the church will at best be a part of your life. If a bride, the church will be the party of your life.

One of my favorite "party pies" is Key lime. A friend from Florida tells of his grandmother's lime tree, which suddenly stopped yielding fruit. After a season of puny, pruny pickings, she sent my friend out into the yard with a baseball bat. Her instructions were clear, albeit severe: "Smack the tree trunk as hard as you can a few times. Shake up the tree. Wake it up. Stir the tree to its roots."

My friend did as he was told. He swung the bat so hard the soles of his feet rocked. The next season there was an effusion of rich, ripe limes—some of the biggest and best the tree had ever produced.

Igniting Passion in Your Church is a baseball bat that can wake the church and shake it to its roots. It's not enough for the church to sing "Hearts unfold like flowers before Thee" ("Joyful, Joyful, We Adore Thee"). The church must bear fruit for a hungry world. A barren fig tree prompted some of the harshest words Jesus ever uttered. Fail to bear fruit, Jesus warned his disciples, and "the kingdom of God will be taken away from you and given to a people who will produce its fruit" (Matthew 21:43). The fruitfulness of the Hillvue Heights tree is evidenced by the fact that I find myself telling more stories about this church than almost any other.

After reading this book, you will too.

Leonard Sweet
Drew Theological School, George Fox University, www.preachingplus.com

Introduction

I am a pastor. But for much of my life, I've had a love/hate relationship with the church. I've loved Jesus and his people, but I've struggled with the institution—the business, the organization, the image—called the church.

This is the story of how God has shown me what the church can be. Of how he gave me an unquenchable fire, a desire for a church that embraces all people—a church that lets them know their lives can change through the grace of Jesus Christ. A place where people are set free, not confined and regulated.

Let me tell you how I discovered God's design for the church and became convinced that she—as the radiant bride of Christ—can captivate the world, beginning with you.

Struggling

God's reveals his remarkable design for the church in Ephesians 5:25-33. In that passage, the church is described as the bride of Christ. What an amazing metaphor! What does it mean? What are its ramifications for us, today, two thousand years after the metaphor was first used?

I've discovered that it means simply and astoundingly this: The church is actively engaged in a relationship with a holy and almighty God, a relationship sparked and maintained by mutual and passionate love.

But do we in the church really know who we are as the bride of Christ? In our attempts at institutionalization, organization, and productivity for God, have we lost our identity as the bride of God's Son? Have we become so preoccupied with the wedding trappings that we've overlooked the Groom?

The path to reigniting the church's passion for Jesus isn't the next program, the next conference, or the next book. White-hot passion in the church begins when we rediscover a love relationship with Jesus and allow that relationship to shape everything we do.

Have we become so preoccupied with the wedding trappings that we've overlooked the Groom?

The church is a living organism, not an inanimate institution or a building. The church's life is the relationship between a committed Groom and a loving bride. And that's what our disconnected world needs to see: a loving bride. A culture disenchanted with cold formality and calculated precision needs a passionate church. The adjectives that'll describe the church of the twenty-first century are *loving, connected, authentic, passionate, real, risky, mysterious, messy, beautiful, brave, fluid, fun,* and *honest.* Does that description scare you? It shouldn't. You're Jesus' bride, and these are marital must-haves. It's time for the church to replace corporate language with passionate language. It's time we say "I do" to Jesus again and leave our business-clad suitors behind.

It's time we say "I do" to Jesus again and leave our business-clad suitors behind.

Journey to the Center of Church Leadership

When I finished high school, I wondered what I might do next. I began to sense that God was urging me to use my life to spread his message. I thought, "Oh, no, please help me—God's going to use me in the church." I struggled with the church's image. I had my own image. I was an adolescent of the '80s in Kentucky. I had long hair, drove a fast car, and listened to loud music. I was a blue-jeans-and-boots-wearing, truck-driving, fun-loving guy. I also loved Jesus, and he loved me. I loved hanging out with people who loved Jesus.

But the church that I saw spelled boredom, captivity, and death. It was full of business meetings, processes, programs, and systems that were either approved or disapproved. It was full of unpleasant images, including the image of the preacher—the stale, stuffy, reserved, conservative-on-all-issues, never-out-of-line, polite, meek, quiet, kind, considerate, inviting-people-to-be-cooperative type of person I knew I could never be.

Even so, God clearly gave me the idea that I was to preach. Don't get me wrong—I didn't mind talking. I didn't mind telling people about Jesus. But I did mind the image of the preacher and the image of the church. I tucked the idea away, thinking God would not call someone with long hair, a goatee, a wild personality, and a loud voice—someone who seemed to create more chaos than peace. Surely God would not use a person like *me* for his church. I told God, "You know, you could use me as a businessman, maybe a lawyer, or maybe a football coach, but not a preacher. Please, Lord, not a preacher."

I bargained with God and offered alternatives, but as the urgings of the Holy Spirit became more insistent, I gave up. Or should I say, "bowed down"?

Even so, instead of embracing the church, living with the church, and being excited about the church, I continued to struggle with my dislike of the church. As I dealt with the mystery of intimacy, I had to confess, before God, that I had never viewed his church as something that related to him. It was a place where people visited him. To live with God, I found, a person had to go outside the walls of the institutionalized church.

To live with God, I found, a person had to go outside the walls of the institutionalized church.

The church where I first worked as a youth and associate pastor (at the age of nineteen) embodied everything I despised about church. It was stuffy. The people didn't like one another. It was full of traditions and unwritten rules and regulations. It was confusing. It was a church that believed in high democracy. In fact, in one business session, the members debated the topic of purchasing toilet paper. I thought, "What in the world are we going to do if the church votes this down? What will be next?" So I raised my hand and asked if I could amend the motion to get rid of the sandpaper-like, industrial-strength toilet paper and move to a softer brand. The moderator did not appreciate my suggestion and said the toilet paper issue was a serious matter. Silenced, I wondered, "Why am I wanting to give my life to this church, to any church?" I saw no life in the church; all I saw was lifeless regulation.

Who Said This Is *My* Church?

I ministered on staff for about nine months, and then I married my bride, Elizabeth. The early years of our marriage and my ministry taught me that I didn't know anything about marriage or the church. Both became a routine. We woke up, went to work, went to school, worked some more, woke up, went to work, went to school, worked some more. I was moving through the marriage system as poorly as I was navigating the church system.

My mentors in the ministry believed that if I followed the rules I might succeed as a church pastor, and they began to train me. For a while I tried to submit to their instruction. I parted my hair on the side, put on my suit and tie, took off my cowboy boots, and shined my shoes. I tried to act like a pastor. This effort resulted in the worst struggle of all. As I became a minister to the church, I lost more than heart and passion. I lost faith. I lost hope. I lost joy. I lost understanding. I lost my bearings. I became depressed and saw the church as useless.

> *As I became a minister to the church, I lost more than heart and passion. I lost faith. I lost hope. I lost joy. I lost understanding. I lost my bearings.*

In the fall of 1987 when I was in my first semester of seminary, I was about to tell the Lord, "No more." Discouraged and disappointed, I cried, "God, if this is your church, I can't take it. I can't be a part of it. I can't give my life to it."

Then the Spirit of God, in a soft, still, powerful whisper, simply responded, "Who said this is *my* church?" Dumbfounded, stunned, mesmerized (possibly even Midas-ized), I pulled my truck to the side of the road. I had actually sensed the Spirit of God speaking. I had heard him. Maybe not audibly, but with ears of the heart, ears of the soul, ears stronger than those of the outward body.

I *knew* it was God. It wasn't my subconscious. It wasn't my imagination. It was God saying, "Who said this is *my* church?"

I said, "I did, Lord. I just said it is your church." As soon as I spoke those words, I thought, *Who am I to tell God what his church is?* I pulled out a little green Gideon New Testament (this is a freebie, a good story for a Gideon speaker to use). God pointed me to Acts 2, and I have never been the same since then.

Passion Point

I invite you to explore God's question, which set me on a quest in 1987: "Who said this is my *church?"*

"Who said this is *my* church?" After hearing this question, I made a request: "Lord Jesus, show me your church." Suddenly I found myself in a new struggle. As God began to show me his church, I realized that, in fighting against protocol, authority, and tradition, I had become bitter and cynical. My passion had turned to anger. I was like a person trapped in quicksand: The more I wiggled and struggled, the more it sucked me under.

Then I realized that trying to change an institution, to reroute a system, wasn't fighting for the right thing. In fact, I hadn't been called to fight at all. I'd been called to love Jesus Christ and to be loved by Jesus Christ. I'd been moved, commissioned, encouraged, placed, and connected as his bride. God loved me, and I was discovering that he loved me enough to show me his church.

In Acts 2, I saw a fervent spirit. I saw God delivering provisions to his people. I saw a group of people who were unmistakably overwhelmed by the living Jesus. *Show me your church, Jesus. Show me your church.* Maybe you need to stop reading right now, go find your Bible, and read Acts 2. Maybe you need to pray, "Show me your church, Jesus. Show me your church."

Show me your church, Jesus. Show me your church.

I encourage you to step back and discover the church within you. You must discover your identity. You're part of the bride, and you are called to become intimate with Jesus. In that holy struggle with intimacy and mystery, new life will emerge.

Jesus in Barren River

My first real pastorate was in a small country church on a hill. When I arrived, I prayed, "Dear God, show me your church. Show me the body of Christ. Show me the bride of Christ. Show me the community of Christ." He did—not with fine things, but with passionate things.

Barren River Baptist Church was a rural church; people tilled the soil and worked in the factories. It was a family and a community. This church never had a vision, except to be there for one another. In fact, the church didn't even have a telephone. But at Barren River Baptist Church, God showed me *his* church.

This church never had a vision, except to be there for one another. In fact, the church didn't even have a telephone. But at Barren River Baptist Church, God showed me his *church.*

At Barren River, I learned to love God's people. I learned to accept new challenges. I learned to preach, to love, to listen, to respect, and to be a part of the community. Barren River will always hold a special place in my heart. It's not a church that would ever be named in Rev Magazine or spotlighted for its success as a great church. But it was there, in that very unexpected location, that I discovered a great, passionate church.

We started there with about fifty people. Eventually, more came. I learned more and more about loving and falling in love with Jesus. People came to change their lives. They came to find healing. They came to be something greater than they had been. It was church.

Instead of having to be kicked out of bed on Sunday mornings, I was up and ready to go. I started the fire in the furnace, opened the door, preached, hugged, sang, listened, and learned. My family and I were the first pastor and family in the history of this church to live in the community with the people. I became known as the preacher on the hill.

I learned to be who I am. I rode my motorcycle, went deer hunting with the folks, and fished the river. I had more conversations about the church while riding a combine or stripping tobacco than while attending deacons' meetings. I led people to Jesus over games of pool at the country store, not through programmed evangelism.

God taught me that every living human being is important to him. My experience at Barren River showed me that the church is God's place of activity and that God has big dreams and never sees impossibilities. I will always be indebted to the people of Barren River for teaching me how to "be church."

Finding God in the Brokenness at Hillvue Heights

I was a pastor at Barren River Baptist Church for three and a half years. But God wanted me to see more of his church. In 1991 he sent me to Hillvue Heights Baptist Church—a broken-down, busted-up, messed-up Baptist church that had lost its way through institutional regulation. This church had more business meetings than prayer meetings.

This place was as wracked by disappointment as I had been in 1987. I walked through empty, dusty hallways. The carpet was torn and tattered. The hollow sanctuary seemed to cry, "Where are those who love me?"

I walked through empty, dusty hallways. The carpet was torn and tattered. The hollow sanctuary seemed to cry, "Where are those who love me?"

Before I was hired, I met with members of the pulpit committee. I looked in their eyes and said, "God's going to make you a great church. People's lives will be changed; they will be healed and developed so that they can make a difference in this world." I was a twenty-six-year-old kid, but I had a vision and a passion from God. They had a church building and a crew of people who had stuck it out. If God put us together, the possibilities would be endless.

After a month of talking, praying, searching, listening, hoping, fearing, and struggling, I became the pastor of Hillvue Heights Baptist Church. We didn't start our church-pastor relationship in the typical way. For one thing, they didn't hear me preach until after I was hired. We decided to be guided by Acts 2 instead of the bylaws. We agreed to forget what was in the past and strive toward what was in the future.

That was twelve years ago. Before my own life changed and God led me to Acts 2, I was broken, empty, and disappointed. I heard the Lord Jesus

Christ saying, "I will fill you with my grace." Now I've seen God turn a broken-down, disappointed, burned-out, busted-up, traditional, highly regulated church into his place of grace. He lifted up his bride and placed this message inside her: "This is a place where everybody can encounter Jesus. This is a place where lives can change, where people can be spiritually healed, and where people can grow, develop, and become what God wants them to become."

Walk the Aisle—the Wedding Aisle

The mystery of the church is that Jesus loves his bride. Jesus loves his bride so much that she will win in the end. She may struggle. She may be tattered. She may be bruised. However, there is a great promise in the Scripture: *He will present her without stain or wrinkle or any other blemish.* As you read the pages of this book, I pray that the Holy Spirit will iron out some of your own wrinkles. If you have stains that you feel are permanent, I pray that through Jesus Christ you'll see them removed.

This book is not another book on how to create another method for the church. This book invites you to struggle, to become a part of a blessed mystery, and to be the church in the world, declaring the hope and glory of God to people who are disappointed, dismayed, and disillusioned.

Passion Point

I hope you're seeing that God did not send me to extravagant places; he sent me to possible places. What are the possible places where you may discover the church within you? What are the possible places where the church may discover Jesus in you?

Wedding Checklist

1. At your next staff meeting, read Ephesians 5:22-33. Ask members of your staff to think about the image of the church as a bride. Ask if they consider it relevant and if they think it is meaningful. Do they see it as challenging?

2. How does the bride identity contrast with the more corporate identities prevalent in the church today?

3. What would change if your church functioned as a bride rather than a business?

4. What do you believe is at the heart of the bride metaphor? Is this at the heart of your church's core identity and mission?

5. What's preventing your church from becoming a church of passion?

Flirting:

Where Passionate Faith Begins

I saw her the first day of my high school years. There she was, in the percussion section—that beautiful, slender girl with long, blonde hair. It wasn't her lovely, blonde hair that got my attention, though, nor her big, brown eyes.

It was that ring on her toe.

I had never seen a toe ring. That unique touch motivated me to speak up as she sashayed my way. I said, "Where did you get that ring on your toe?"

She shot back, "And who are you?"

"My name's Steve Ayers," I said.

She said, "So?"

I went on to fifth period, and there she was again. Now a gym sneaker covered up that ring on her toe. Since oral communication hadn't worked so well, I tried nonverbal communication. I took off my purple Converse Chuck Taylor All Star shoe and gently pitched it toward her, thinking it would land beside her and she'd turn around and glance my way.

I missed. Instead of landing beside her, my shoe hit her head. She asked one of my best friends, "Who *is* that guy?" At that moment I certainly didn't think she would someday be my wife, and she definitely didn't think of me as husband material. But our future had started. There was a connection. It all started with flirting.

How to Be a Flirting Church

The church needs to learn how to flirt. We need to get the world to flirt with the Groom. We need to inspire people to ask, "Will Jesus connect with me?" Instead of flirting with methodologies, consumerism, and the serve-me attitude, we should be flirting with Jesus Christ—and we should be helping others flirt too.

Instead of flirting with methodologies, consumerism, and the serve-me attitude, we should be flirting with Jesus Christ—and we should be helping others flirt too.

Flirting is that initial process of signaling your attraction to someone. When you flirt, you send the message "Hey, I'm interested." You might even send the message "Hey, I'm interesting." The church needs to do both.

If we're going to be Christ-followers and Christ-lovers, we need to quit glancing at Jesus and open our eyes fully to his grace, love, joy, and peace. We need to fix our gaze so completely on Jesus Christ that we cause the world to look where we're looking. Everything we do needs to say, "Hey, I'm interested, and I know I'm interesting." Spiritual flirtation. Intriguing, isn't it? Let's explore how to do it.

The Attractive Power of Passion

We often hear people comment about the folks at Hillvue Heights, "Those people *believe* that stuff. They really believe it."

Three years into my ministry here, I asked a woman who came up to me after the service, "So how was church today? What was it like?"

She replied, "I just can't come back."

I know that Hillvue isn't for everyone, and we really try to connect people with a church that's right for their circumstances and life experience. So I said, "Really? Help me to help others. Why can't you come back?"

"I'm not looking for a church that gets this serious. I'm looking for a church that I can just go to," she said.

Her comments made me feel sad for her, but they helped us understand something about ourselves—our passion is

Passion Point

Think for just a moment. What does your church really believe in? What are you flirting with? Styles and methods? Procedures and processes? Do you believe that what you're doing is the will of God? Is the ministry a show to draw a crowd? Or is it an invitation to flirt with Jesus?

noticeable. And that's a positive thing.

People are attracted to those who are serious about their beliefs. People with passionate beliefs become unstoppable in their mission and influence. If the church is going to cause people to flirt with Jesus, she needs to get passionate about Jesus.

People with passionate beliefs become unstoppable in their mission and influence.

Where's Your Eye?

Glancing, gazing, and even gawking are all part of the flirtation process.

Think for a moment about the church you're serving or are a part of. What is it gazing at?

Many churches are glaring at the problems. Problems always seem to get our undivided attention. We fix our attention on a lack of people, a lack of money, and a lack of enthusiasm in the church. We also glare at people's unwillingness to seize the future, to change, or to worship fervently. Are problems diverting your attention from your passion?

We need to quit glaring at what seem to be impossibilities and start peering at possibilities. Philippians 3:4-7 helps us to understand that human efforts are not sufficient to advance the cause of Christ. The abilities to articulate a vision, organize, structure, motivate, and engage are all part of our call, but they are not at the *core* of church.

Paul learned that his impressive resume and experiences gained him nothing compared to the surpassing joy of knowing Christ, the fellowship of his suffering, and the power of his resurrection. Paul was willing to join in Christ's suffering so he might *know* the power of the resurrected Christ.

We've been a church, at least in the last fifty years, that has only glanced at our Christ-centered potential while focusing on the impossibilities that threaten to overwhelm us. We're intended to do just the opposite.

Do They See Jesus?

As we think about what we're staring at inside the church, we ought also to know what the world is seeing inside the church. Are people outside the church even giving the church a glance? Are they flirting? Are we helping them flirt?

Research by George Barna informs us that the church is not relevant to our culture.[1] One of the church's most critical problems is that we've become *so* irrelevant that the world doesn't even want to glance at us. Maybe if we'd quit glaring at impossibilities, the world might start glancing at the possibilities of a relationship with Jesus Christ.

We need to structure and empower our churches based on the power of Jesus' cross and resurrection. That kind of power, which knows no limitations, will get the world flirting with us. As long as the church allows itself to be confined by human limitations, the world will not be impressed. It won't glance our way. We need to release Jesus' power in our churches.

We need to structure and empower our churches based on the power of Jesus' cross and resurrection. That kind of power, which knows no limitations, will get the world flirting with us.

Do you remember the days when you were deeply intrigued by someone? Love does odd things to us. It makes us do unusual things. It causes us to experience strange, new feelings. Sometimes those feelings are warm; sometimes they're uncertain; other times they're definitely certain. There's up; there's down. There are even turnarounds. Do you see this pattern in your church?

How are you helping people fall in love with Jesus? Think about the sermons that have been preached and the songs that have been sung in your church. Think about how people are welcomed into your congregation. Think about the people in the corridors of the church building. Think about how the parking lot fills up, and picture the parking lot after services. Do people linger? Do they experience community? Or do they make a quick exit because a glance is all they need to know that there is nothing in your church that attracts them? Or maybe people discover that they're not ready to engage the truth.

In any case, we're not just representatives of Jesus; it goes much deeper than that. When we *know* Jesus, we show people who he is and what he's about. What are people seeing? Are we inspiring them to flirt with Jesus?

We need to refocus on Jesus. The Bible declares that we're to have no other gods before God; it's the first commandment (Exodus 20:3). Jesus said, "I and the Father are one" (John 10:30). Jesus tells us he's the way, the truth, and the life (John 14:6). Paul wrote that the church is a bride connected to the Groom (Ephesians 5:25-33). John said that we will drink from the river of life because we've been connected to the Lamb (Revelation 22:1-5). It's all about Jesus. Nothing more. Nothing less.

It's easy for us to *state* that our focus is on Jesus. But it's often tough to *be* focused on Jesus in the midst of problems. If we maintain our passion for Jesus, we'll always be going in the right direction. When a church is Jesus-focused and studying the possibilities, the church—through Christ—naturally becomes a loving community. Churches that walk in the power of the risen Christ inevitably walk in the love of the redeeming Savior.

Churches that walk in the power of the risen Christ inevitably walk in the love of the redeeming Savior.

What Are Our Toe Rings?

What attracted me most to that young lady who later became my wife was her uniqueness. She was secure enough to wear a toe ring when nobody else was wearing a toe ring. I've found that what's most intriguing is not what everybody else is doing, but what a few are doing.

In Jesus' world, the religious experts were practicing condemnation. But Jesus was practicing grace. Think about the story of the woman caught in adultery (John 8:1-11). The Pharisees came to trap Jesus. What did Jesus do? He wrote something on the ground with his finger. The Pharisees left. They had no more questions after Jesus said, "If any one of you is without sin, let him be the first to throw a stone at her." They all realized who they were. They were sinners.

Then Jesus released the woman, saying, "Woman, where are they? Has no one condemned you?"

She said, "No one, sir."

Passion Point

Now, let's think for a moment. What's your church's focus? Is it to draw a crowd? Is it to tell the crowd about Jesus? Is it to become so involved with Jesus in your own individual lives that the rest is natural? Is your church all about Jesus?

He said, "Then neither do I condemn you. Go now and leave your life of sin." That was unique! The woman could leave her old life because she had been introduced to a new life.

As our church grew, we constantly asked, "What is our identity? Who are we going to be?" In essence, we were asking, "What does the world need us to be?" Wrong question. The wrong questions lead to the wrong answers.

The main question to ask in establishing any church's identity is, Who are we in Christ? We had to change our focus.

The main question to ask in establishing any church's identity is, Who are we in Christ?

As we stop focusing on who *we* are and begin setting our sights on who *Jesus* is, we activate his power in our churches. It's Jesus who makes us unique. If we're going to get the world to flirt with the church, we need to feature our ultimate uniqueness—Jesus. Seeing Jesus in us will cause people to ask us who we are.

The church is unique, but we don't seem to realize the potential inherent in that uniqueness. As we evangelize, reach out, and seek to influence the world, our uniqueness causes people to glance at us. Can you imagine what kindness, simple courtesy, politeness, a handshake, a hug, a smile, or encouragement can do? These actions sound so elementary and simple, but don't forget that it's the elementary aspects of life that usually lead people into a relationship with Jesus.

Let's rediscover and celebrate what's really unique about us.

The Uniqueness of Our Caring

Steve Sjogren maintains that evangelism can be spearheaded in the world by simply being kind.[2] When I recently visited New York City, I talked to everyone. I naturally interact with people wherever I am. One of the reasons people responded to me was that I spoke when we were supposed to be silent. Many people were intrigued when I said simply, "How are you doing? Hey, what's up?" (They could tell by my accent that I was certainly not from New York!) Some would smile back in response; some glanced at me and then walked on. But everyone had to wonder, Who *is* this guy?

No one has ever come to Hillvue Heights Church because of my great theological mind. Rather, people say, "I met somebody, and he was kind."

Our pastor of pastoral care, Mark Hale, has seen people receive Jesus in their lives and be totally changed because someone handed them a sandwich in a hospital room and said, "We care about you." Sometimes when Mark goes to the hospital to minister to families that are part of the church, he also brings lunch for everybody in the waiting area. He says simply, "We just want you to know that we are a church that cares."

Caring should be one of the church's hallmarks, but we too often forget to care. I'm not suggesting that we become a "mushy" church. I'm talking real, Christlike caring, not momentary politeness. I'm talking about caring that people get connected to God for eternity. Caring for others, no matter who they are, tells them that they, too, can be connected with Jesus Christ. Caring for others allows people to understand that Jesus cares for them. Have we forgotten that? Have we lost the art of caring?

Caring should be one of the church's hallmarks, but we too often forget to care.

We can care for others in very simple ways. In the South, especially in many towns in the rural South, the Wal-Mart Supercenter is the hub of the community. The lines are usually fifteen or twenty people deep at the cash register. People standing in the lines typically get frustrated, so it really blows them away when someone in front of them says, "Go ahead. Go in front of me." We call that waiting-in-line evangelism. The gesture shows people that we care, that we know that their time is important and their lives are important. People rarely turn down the offer. Caring for people causes them to flirt with the possibilities Jesus might introduce in their lives.

The Uniqueness of Our Spirit

The church is unique in another way. The church is attractive because the Spirit is attractive. The Holy Spirit lives inside us. The Spirit has reshaped us, has remade us, and constantly guides us. Think about how this unique ingredient could begin to attract people to your church community.

Notice that I've been talking about drawing people to the church in a lot of ways that don't cost a dime. If you'll gaze steadfastly at Jesus, if you'll be immersed in Jesus, if you'll realize your connection to Jesus, and if you'll begin demonstrating Christlike kindness, caring, and attractiveness, fruit will emerge from your ministry. Those who are loving, joyful, peaceful, patient, kind, good, faithful, gentle, and self-controlled (see Galatians 5:22-23) attract people who want to have the same qualities.

The Uniqueness of Our Faith

We are also unique in that our relationship to Christ drives us to be faithful. Faithfulness activates faith. Faithfulness illustrates faith. Brave, bold faith causes the world to glance our way.

My wife, Elizabeth, is faithful to other people. The other day, she picked up our son, Blake, after his seventh-grade basketball game and dropped him off at my office so he could finish a project. Then she drove back across town to pick up one of Blake's teammates, who had been asked to stay and play in the eighth-grade game. This boy is a dear friend, a twelve-year-old who's never had any consistency in his life. He's never known the faithfulness of an adult. When Elizabeth met him after his game, he said, "You're here to pick me up, even though Blake's not here?"

She said, "I'm here because I told you I would be here." What a marvelous moment! What a grace connection. What an illustration of the bride of Christ. We're to be actively and practically faithful so that when the world does glance, it will see Jesus.

The Uniqueness of Our Purpose

As the bride, we're also unique because we're a people of purpose. Our lives are about the Great Commandment and the Great Commission. We're called to love Jesus with all that we are—heart, soul, and mind—and then dare to love our neighbors as we love ourselves (Matthew 22:37-40). And we're called to take this love to the ends of the earth in Jesus' name (Matthew 28:19-20).

As we embrace and practice our purpose, we become an illustration of Jesus. There's no doubt about it: When we become intrigued with God's purpose, we'll activate God's principles.

There's no doubt about it: When we become intrigued with God's purpose, we'll activate God's principles.

The purpose of the church is to reveal the nature of the relationship that Jesus has given us. Being in Christ allows us to share Jesus with the world. Our purpose is not about *doing;* our purpose is to love Jesus in worship, live out his teachings, and illustrate his love to the world.

The Uniqueness of Our Changed Lives

The church is not without struggles, flaws, mistakes, mishaps, and failures. We need to expose them.

I am quick to honestly share my own mistakes with the congregation. One Saturday I was asked to sit in the stands instead of coach the remainder of a football game because I had a not-so-holy moment. The next day, I told our congregation about my failure and what they would probably hear in the community. The religious pony express had already circulated the rumor, but I told my congregants about the incident just in case they wanted to hear my less juicy version. I did apologize for losing my cool, and I admitted that it was wrong (even though I had a videotape to prove my point to the referees). Some laughed; others were relieved that the story wasn't quite as bad as the one they had previously heard.

But the most surprising reaction came from a man who had been attending Hillvue Heights Church for months but hadn't yet given his life to Jesus. He did so on this particular Sunday. I asked him, "Why today?"

He said, "I finally believe that Jesus is real and true because, if you are honest enough to reveal your imperfections, then I believe you are telling the truth about Jesus, too."

We at Hillvue Heights Church don't ask people to come and be perfect; we ask people to come and join in a relationship with Christ. This relationship of grace transforms and redevelops their lives. The bottom line in a church is changed lives.

I've seen people at Hillvue trade in their old lives and change. One person whose spouse had recently experienced a life change at Hillvue called and said, "My husband isn't the same person."

I thought, "Is this person going to be upset?"

Instead she said, "Can I get it too?"

Life change is an attractor. It's a draw.

Passion Point

What is going on in your church? Jesus intrigued people. Do you?

The Uniqueness of Our Heat

When the church truly focuses on Jesus, it automatically begins to flirt with the world. Revelation 3:14-16 tells us that the greatest crisis in the church at Laodicea was that it was neither hot nor cold. It was "kinda." I don't see a whole lot of people attracted to kinda people. Some days they're kinda with God, and some days they're not. They kinda believe, and then they kinda don't.

I don't see a whole lot of people attracted to kinda people. Some days they're kinda with God, and some days they're not. They kinda believe, and then they kinda don't.

The Bible calls us to be hot for God. If we're turned on for God, we'll become alluring, because people will say, "I want to have what they have. I think I want to investigate the possibilities of Jesus. I'll flirt with those possibilities." Heat draws people to Christ; lukewarm (kinda) drives them away.

Lukewarm churches are usually people-pleasing churches. Second Timothy 4 tells us that in the last days, there will be a multitude—many, a crowd—that will be drawn to doctrine that tells them only what they want to hear. Church leaders need to constantly guard the focus of their agendas. *What* are we presenting? *Who* are we presenting? The question of *why* we are presenting something should always be a part of our leadership evaluation. Each ministry should boldly attract people to come, to experience, and to connect with Jesus Christ.

Every ministry in the church and every move the church makes can attract people to Jesus Christ. Help your people understand that a smile in the worship service is an important element of worship and that hanging around *after* the worship experience may be the ultimate worship experience.

One of the greatest ministries we have at Hillvue is what I call the hang-around ministry. It's not one of our official ministries, but it's one of the most effective. People hang around the parking lot. They hang around the lobbies. They hang around the worship center. They talk. They listen. They share their experiences. They wonder. They dream. They conceive ideas. They make connections. They see possibilities. Those who hang around with people who are hot in their relationship with God become curious about what a relationship with God could do for them. We need to become hot—boiling hot—for the things of God.

The Uniqueness of Our Passion

You've probably met passionate people. It doesn't matter what they're passionate about; it could be golf, motorcycles, or yachts. The passion that oozes from them makes you wonder, "Hmm. I wonder what makes them tick. Why are they so involved? Why are they like that?"

The church needs to make a move. We've got to dive below the surface of just hoping God will do great things in our lives to *becoming* the great things of God. Let's not miss it, church. We *are* the great relationship of an almighty God. We *are* the lovers of Jesus Christ. We need to be passionate about showing the world that Jesus Christ is our ultimate lover. As we move beyond surface religion into eternal relationship, we explode with the intimacy, passion, fascination, hope, love, and joy of that relationship.

The church needs to make a move. We've got to dive below the surface of just hoping God will do great things in our lives to **becoming** *the great things of God.*

Passionate people always intrigue others. We're the bride of Christ. It's not possible to be more loved than we are. So why are we so blasé? Satan himself is most effective when he prevents us, through deception, from passionately realizing and celebrating who we are.

The Uniqueness of Our Worship

Like many other churches, Hillvue debated about whether to use a traditional or a more fervent style of worship. We came to the conclusion that the best thing we could do is worship passionately. We've found that those who worship passionately intrigue those who are never in church. Jesus loves the church with great passion, so we ought to return that passion in worship.

Why not be so radiant that the world is curious about us, instead of us being curious about the world? Our worship should be such that people ask us, "What's the matter with you?" I pray we have experiences in our church that match the experience of the people in Capernaum who saw the paralyzed man released and freed (Mark 2). After that miracle, people exclaimed, "We have never seen anything like this! We have never seen anything like this!" What if our congregations, our worship, and our teaching become so intriguing that people say about us, "We've never seen anything like this"?

What's Your Line?

Part of flirting is learning how to give a great presentation. This requires that we first ask, What are we presenting? Are we presenting who we are—our organization, our institution, our structures, and our traditions—or are we inviting the world to embrace a relationship with Jesus Christ? Far too often, we expend less effort inviting people to Jesus Christ than we do inviting them to our organization. We need to be clear that the church is about being connected to Jesus.

Far too often, we expend less effort inviting people to Jesus Christ than we do inviting them to our organization. We need to be clear that the church is about being connected to Jesus.

We must be careful, because it's easy to turn the church inward. The desire to take care of people can lead us to avoid connecting with God. If people's needs drive our ministry, then we forget that the ultimate need and the ultimate connection is Jesus Christ. Ray Anderson, referring to Jesus' ministry, states, "His ministry is first of all directed to God and not to the world. The needs of the world are

Passion Point

Take a moment to really think about your church. When people who are in the world look through your stained glass, your clear windows, the windows of your inner-city building or your metal building, or the windows of your home, what do they see? Do they see passion? Do they hear love? Can they feel movement? If so, they'll begin to knock gently on the door. "Can I come and see? Can I come and hear? Will you welcome me?"

I pray that we'll welcome them. It's that flirtatious wink or glance that could be the first step into a relationship with Jesus. That wink could lead someone to becoming part of the bride. That question could lead to a changed life.

35

recognized and brought into this ministry, but they do not set the agenda."[3]

When people flirt, it's because someone got their attention. It's because someone attracted them. It is amazing; Jesus gets people's attention. I've heard it more than once. "Preacher, the reason I come to this church is because you talk about Jesus. I know as long as you're talking about Jesus, we'll be going in the right direction." I've found that if we're confidently convinced that Jesus is truly the one who will change the world, then the world will begin to look toward Jesus. Our message is, Come and see. Come and touch. Come and taste. Come and experience.

Freedom to Flirt

As we encourage the church to flirt, we must constantly try to remember what it's like to enter church for the first time—to not understand the songs, to be intrigued but not know the ropes. One of the greatest errors we can make after becoming established is to forget to flirt, to forget that there are many others who still aren't established.

I've forgotten what it's like to be single because I've been married longer than I was single. The same is true of the church. Because we've been connected for so long, some of us have forgotten what it was like to flirt with the possibility that God might connect with us.

A Model Bride

The smells of summer always remind me of my grandmother. Summer meant that we would go to her house. Piled in that old station wagon, we headed for Meridian, Mississippi, where I was embraced by a beautiful bride who had celebrated more than fifty years of marriage. She knew how to welcome people. She was always kind. She was always caring. She *always* presented herself attractively.

My grandmother never glared at her problems. Earlier in her life, a disease had caused her to lose her hearing. Even so, she continued to hear those she loved by embracing them. Her hands were crippled by arthritis, but she didn't stop playing the church organ.

The church needs to model this kind of attitude. Despite our problems, we must reach out and tell the world that there's hope in Christ. This is the unique and intriguing message of the church.

Is Flirting the Goal?

No! Flirting is where authentic relationship begins, but flirting will not bring a church into deep commitment. We'll never become a part of the bride if all we do is flirt. But flirting is where connection to Jesus begins.

After his disciples walked with Jesus intimately for three years, Jesus blessed them and said, "Go now, and tell others. Tell the world. Tell the nations. Tell the people."

The deeper we grow with Jesus, the more we're moved to invite those on the perimeter who are just beginning to flirt with the possibilities. Those who dare will open their arms in hospitality to those who gather in the back rows, balconies, and sidewalks and even to those who stand at a distance, waiting, wondering, glancing. I hope we can look back. I hope we can wink. I hope we can walk by and say, "Hi. How are you? Would you like to come? Would you like to hear?"

Passion Point

Now, think for a moment. How intrigued are you about being a part of worship every Sunday? Ask yourself, "Where is the intriguing message? Where's the message of possibility? Where's the message of hope?" Sometimes we lose the message of the Groom because we try so hard to present what only Jesus himself can present.

Wedding Checklist

1. What is the extent of your church's influence in the unchurched world?

2. Is your church equipped to help people flirt safely?

3. Think about the first time you met your spouse. How can you help people have that kind of experience when they meet Jesus?

4. Think honestly about your church. Has it grown inward? If so, what will it take to become an outward-focused church?

5. How can you intrigue the world by more passionately celebrating the uniqueness of your identity in Christ?

Dating:
Where Passionate Faith Steps Forward

I have a daughter. She's only nine years old, but I know the day is coming when she'll ask that dreaded question: "Daddy, can I go out with so-and-so?" I dread that question because I know that dating entails risk. I won't be able to control the people she'll be with, where they'll go, and what they'll do.

Church, we must prepare to date. When we date, we go *out* to get *in* a relationship. We need to go out into the world to get the world into a relationship with Jesus. The church ought to be a matchmaker. Have you ever thought about evangelism as matchmaking? We have the beautiful responsibility to invite people to go out with Jesus. We need to get *out* there so people may *connect* with Jesus.

When we date, we go out *to get* in *a relationship.*

Passion Point

Think about your church. Is it willing to become a matchmaker? Is it willing to go to those who are disconnected and set them up on a date with Jesus?

Are you willing to say to Joe, Sally, Sue, or whomever, "I know a guy named Jesus who would like to go out with you"? The churches that learn to ask people to go out with Jesus are the churches that begin to change the communities around them. The crucial thing is that we must stop being afraid to ask. The Bible tells us that we don't have because we don't ask (James 4:2).

In asking us to engage our communities, God is simply asking us to connect people with Jesus. Unfortunately, we often invite people out on the wrong date. We ask people everything *except* to consider a connection with Jesus.

The Art of Invitation

Many people attend church today just to see what's going on. They're content to sit up in the balcony—to remain on the sidelines. Jesus is never content with that. Jesus saw Zacchaeus watching from a tree, but obviously that wasn't enough. He said, "I'm going to your house today, Zacchaeus. We're going out." Today, the church is more likely to make Zacchaeus comfortable up in his tree than to ask him to come down and make a connection with Jesus.

Today, the church is more likely to make Zacchaeus comfortable up in his tree than to ask him to come down and make a connection with Jesus.

Connecting people with Jesus isn't about comfort; it's about changing lives. Jesus isn't connecting with us so we'll have a better earthly experience. He's calling us to connect with the reality of God, not just the possibility of God. And he's calling the church to bring the world into a connection with God. We can't settle into being a flirting church. We must become a dating church.

Dating is being out there with the people, connecting with the people—not showing the people *your* personhood, but showing them how the personhood of Jesus has connected to you. It's inviting people to a new life.

Passion Point

Does your church do all it can to ensure that those who are disconnected are connected with Jesus? Does it dream the dreams and see the possibilities of God? Does it eventually ask people to come and connect to Jesus, or does it just talk about what the church could be if it did? If your church only dreams about what it would look like if it asked people to engage with Jesus, it's stuck in the flirting mode.

41

The corporate model of the church invites people to come and participate in the systematic programming of a particular church structure. There's nothing wrong with structure. However, church structure is meaningless if we don't allow the personal nature of Jesus to connect with us. This sounds so obvious, yet we often miss it in the church. Too many times, we invite people to our *church* instead of to *Jesus*. That's a tragic mistake.

Too many times, we invite people to our church *instead of to* Jesus. *That's a tragic mistake.*

Passion Point

Has your church mastered the art of invitation? What does your church invite people to do? Does it ask them to come to worship? Does it ask them to come and listen? Does it ask them to experience Jesus Christ?

When people see others having a life-changing experience, they'll want to know what's happened. Several individuals in our congregation have become evangelists without knowing it. People ask them, "What's happened to you?" They respond by inviting people to explore the possibility of what Jesus could do in them. That's an invitation. We invite people to a life change, not to a system or to *our* scene.

Intentional Invitation

Our invitation to Christ needs to be intentional. We'll never see people become a part of the bride of Christ until we *ask* them to. We also need to model and to express what's going on in our lives. In a country song, George Strait sings, "You look so good in love."[1] That's what we want the world to say about us. We need to help others see the effect Jesus' love would have on them.

Think again about Jesus' encounter with Zacchaeus. It wasn't a structured encounter. It wasn't entirely an intellectual or a philosophical encounter. It was an opportunity to be absorbed in the experience and atmosphere of an intimate dinner with Jesus. And look at the response. Zacchaeus' life was utterly changed.

God constantly invites us to continue the journey with Jesus. God invites us to encounter level after level, experience after experience, story after story. He builds intimacy with us. Inviting others is exposing them to that intimacy.

Passion Point

Think about ways your church can invite people to Jesus. Is the invitation intentional or unintentional?

Introducing Jesus

I don't know about you, but in my life, especially when I was a young married person, I sometimes forgot to introduce my wife. This failing made my wife feel worthless, and it made me appear ashamed of her. Jesus has introduced us to the Father. He has said, "If you are not ashamed of me, I will not be ashamed of you before my Father" (Matthew 10:32-33, paraphrased).

We introduce those we love. We're to introduce Jesus to the world. We're to ask the world to experience not only the possibilities of faith but also intimacy with Jesus.

Which is more important: inviting people to Jesus or inviting them to church? When are we going to trust that an experience with Jesus is more overwhelming than an experience with the church? People don't need to meet my process, my tradition, my history, or me. They also don't need to meet you. They need to meet the living Lord, the Spirit of Jesus, the truth of Jesus, and the way of Jesus.

Which is more important: inviting people to Jesus or inviting them to church?

Part of dating is learning to ask the question. I'll say it again. *Ask the question.* One of the church's biggest problems is that it doesn't ask the important questions: Do you know Jesus? Do you know who he is? Do you know what he might do? Would you like to go out with him?

After people are asked those questions, the Holy Spirit takes the next step. Evangelism, discipleship, encountering Jesus, developing in Jesus, faith formation, transformation—whatever you want to call it—does not occur until the person has accepted the invitation. But this acceptance doesn't happen in an instant. It's a process.

Have you accepted that you and Jesus need to hang out together constantly? Maybe your prayer life needs to turn into a date time. Maybe you need to realize that Jesus desires to have fun with you. He desires to have dinner with you. He desires to live life with you.

Jesus is with us all the time. We must accept his presence. You see, when we accept that Jesus is with us because we are his bride, then we can invite others to be with him also.

Accepting the Invitation

Accepting an earthly date can be scary. It automatically invokes fear. What should I say? How should I act? I wonder what she'll discover about me and what I'll discover about her. I wonder if she'll like me. What if she rejects me? And of course, we ask superficial questions as well: Does my hair look OK? Is this the right shirt? Did I wear the right jeans? Whatever the question, the underlying fear is that we'll be rejected if we say yes to the invitation.

It's important for the church to be a bride that accepts people. The greatest strength of Hillvue Heights Church is that it accepts people where they are so that they can encounter Jesus and become what only Jesus can make them. All people can come—people who smoke and drink, people who've not experienced God, and people who have had negative experiences with the church. That's not to say that we do not challenge sinful lifestyles and call people to Christlike living. But our dating principle is, *Accept people where they are.*

This mentality flows from the realization that Jesus has accepted us. People constantly struggle with a fear of rejection. But Jesus tells us it's an unnecessary fear. "I am with you always to the very end of the age" (Matthew 28:20). Fear not. Jesus loves us. We are his. Knowing Jesus' love allows us to ask the world to come and be embraced by Jesus.

Dating is uncomfortable, especially the first date. Who knows what the person will be like? So when people are taking those first steps toward a connection or a date with Jesus, don't make the experience too heavy. People don't go out on a first date and say, "Hey, I'd like to marry you." People explore, seek, look, listen, and discover. Help them do those things with Jesus.

People don't go out on a first date and say, "Hey, I'd like to marry you." People explore, seek, look, listen, and discover. Help them do those things with Jesus.

An unbelieving friend and I have water-skied together for eighteen years, and he's been dating Jesus for about the same number of years. Every summer he brings up something that prompts me to ask him if he's considering connecting to Jesus. He still hasn't said yes to the invitation, but he's exploring the possibility. He never shuns or avoids a conversation about Jesus; he's seeking the truth. He's seeing that a relationship with Jesus is consistent and authentic and that Jesus loves him where he is. The only churches that he has experienced tell him that he isn't worthy and that he must change before he can get a date with Jesus.

Boldly invite people to date Jesus; you've no reason to fear. When I speak to youth groups across the country, I ask what it's like to speak about Jesus to their classmates. They say, "If we stand up and talk about Jesus, they'll say all kinds of things about us." I ask how many people have ever said anything about them for speaking about Jesus. They say, "No one."

We think that our culture will reject Jesus, but people are not rejecting Jesus. They are rejecting the clothes we have placed on him and the conditions he's not responsible for. Most people are rejecting *their image* of Jesus, but they are willing to listen to and possibly date the Jesus of Scripture.

Accepting people where they are also means accepting people with unsavory habits. In our particular Southern culture, smoking cigarettes is not taboo, but it's frowned upon by some. It's not a healthy habit, and our church does not recommend it. However, we don't reject people because they smoke. We don't tell people who have a drinking problem that they'll have to get sober before they can connect with Jesus. Jesus meets us where we are.

The bride needs to show people acceptance. This acceptance is not the kind that promotes destructive habits; it's the kind of acceptance that leads to connection with Jesus, which leads to changed lives. We accept people in order to get them into the process.

The number one reason that non-Christians have come to Hillvue Heights Church over the past ten years is that they know they can come to our church as they are and hear about Jesus. We're not a seeker-sensitive church; we're a Spirit-driven church. We hope that the Holy Spirit catches people. The Spirit will introduce them to the person of Jesus, who tells them that they're accepted and that they can experience changed lives.

Tragically, the church as a whole tends to reject more than it accepts. We immediately frown upon people who don't fit into *our* paradigm or *our* cultural expectations. As a result, we've excluded different races and ethnic groups instead of intentionally connecting with them. Jesus is into people, no matter who they are or where they've been. Exclusion always leads to the chaos of misunderstanding. Let's not mutter about sins; let's show where the solution to sin is. It's in Christ Jesus.

Are you going to invite people to allow Jesus to have dinner with them? Jesus probably could have convinced Zacchaeus right there on the road that he was the Messiah, but instead he went to his house. He took Zacchaeus from a distant place to an intimate place. Shouldn't this be the pattern of the bride of Christ? God's invitation prompts us to move from distant places to intimate places. Come and discover. Come and be connected. Come and be renewed. Come and be changed. Come and be spiritually healed. Come and be remade. This is the language of passion.

Come and discover. Come and be connected. Come and be renewed. Come and be changed. Come and be spiritually healed. Come and be remade. This is the language of passion.

What Makes a Good Date?

Our objective isn't just to date; it's to date well. Consider what makes a good date between a man and a woman. Many of the same principles apply to spiritual dating. Let's look at some of them.

Warm Conversation

One of the most exciting things about dating is finding a person who listens. At least a dozen times, Proverbs implores us to listen: "O listen, my son. O listen, my people." If we're going to invite people to go out with Jesus, we must start listening to them.

Passion Point

What do people experience when they visit your church? Think about the exciting dates you've had. I'll bet the person was interesting and fun and had a sense of humor. Maybe your date offered an intellectual challenge. Certainly, the experience was alluring; it piqued your curiosity. And there was probably romance and some form of passion. Does your church offer these things to those it's dating?

Jesus heard Zacchaeus, even though he hadn't spoken a word. Jesus spoke first, not because Jesus was an extrovert, but because he was illustrating the message that he is here to seek, save, and change those who are lost and disconnected.

Intrigue

We need to understand and revel in the fact that we're an intriguing people, a peculiar people. I told you about my initial attraction to my wife: She wore a toe ring before toe rings had been heard of. That intrigued me. We in the church can intrigue those looking for God's love by being the unique people God created us to be and by reflecting God's love.

I remember celebrating J.R. and Libby's fiftieth anniversary with them. As J.R. watched his wife walk up the aisle to renew their vows, I saw passion, fire, and intimacy in the faces of both.

Later I asked J.R., "Didn't you go through the Great Depression?"

He said, "Yeah, but she was with me."

"What about war?"

"I came back home, and she was waiting for me."

"What's the secret?"

"We've had our bad times. We've had our good times. We were together and we loved each other in all of those times."

That's not a storybook romance; that's the reality of an authentic relationship. The same is true of my experience with the church. I've had rough times as a believer. I've had blissful times as a believer. But Jesus has always been there. Jesus intrigues us because he's always there, always loving us. Dating is learning to be there, just as Jesus is.

Want to know what really intrigues people? It's the loving, joyful, and peaceful nature of Jesus and his bride. We call it the LJP factor in our church. We evaluate all of our ministry events by asking the following questions: Did it reflect the loving nature of God? Did it reflect the joyful nature of God? Did it reflect the peaceful nature of God? When all three factors—love, joy, and peace—were there, we know the event was a good date. People come back to places that are loving, joyful, and peaceful.

Surprise

I love taking my wife out on dates and not telling her where we're going or what we're going to do. Enjoyable surprises intrigue her. As we discover new places and new things, we discover new things about each other.

Are you willing, in your marriage to Christ, to continue to discover new things? Or has your marriage to Christ become routine?

Here are some surprises people have experienced in our church:

Diversity. Nobody can figure out how so many different types of people can be under one roof and still get along.

Honesty. People can't figure out how we can be boldly truthful yet loving at the same time.

Acceptance. People have a hard time figuring out how we can accept sinners and hate sin.

Celebration. People think Jesus is critical, not celebratory. Surprise them by showing that Jesus is the joy of the world.

> *Passion Point*
>
> *Think about the intriguing dates you've experienced. Did they contain an element of spontaneity? What intrigues people about your church? Some of our churches are so programmed that they plan their spontaneity!*

Creativity

When you're dating, you'll need to do more than go to dinner, catch a movie, have minimal conversation, and then say goodnight each time you go out if you want to really get to know someone. Our churches need to be more creative in the ways they connect with people. Don't go at it the same way every time. Don't go to the same place and experience the same date each time. Get creative.

Interest in Others

Have you ever dated people who talked only about themselves? Didn't you get sick and tired of hearing their stories? The church talks too much about itself. It should be inviting people to tell *their* stories. Jesus didn't interrupt Zacchaeus when he was telling his story. Jesus listened. Are we listening to those we're dating?

The church talks too much about itself. It should be inviting people to tell their stories.

We can easily lose our spouses over time if we fail to listen to them and realize how they're changing. We must listen to our congregations, too. It's tough to pastor a church without being involved with its people. It's hard to be a good shepherd if you don't know anything about sheep. It's hard to farm if you're never willing to get dirty. We have to be in the middle of it all, not standing by and just writing about it. We've got to be in the middle of our people's lives, listening, expressing, and connecting.

Good Food

Many good dates include a visit to an exquisite restaurant to eat fine food. Can we understand that communion with God is the beginning of eating the finest food and drinking the finest drink? Jesus is the living water. Jesus turns water into wine. Jesus dines with sinners like Zacchaeus. And Jesus calls his bride to remember him through food and drink.

Every time my lips touch the Communion cup, I am reminded that God is having a conversation with me, another date with me. He's reminding me that by his blood I have been changed, and it is only by his blood that my lips can drink from this cup. Henri Nouwen states, "Drinking the cup that Jesus drank is living a life in and with the spirit of Jesus, which is the spirit of unconditional love. The intimacy between Jesus and Abba, his Father, is an intimacy of complete trust...It is only love."[2]

In Communion Jesus says, "Eat bread, and understand that I was broken for you. I am your substance. I am your life. Eat well. Drink well."

Warning—Jesus dines in unacceptable places. He eats with people who offend the religious and the modern-day Pharisees. He dines with and intrigues sinners, and they desire to come back and eat again. He knows who they are, and he listens to them.

Evaluation

Every date ends with an evaluation. Will we date again? Is this person worth a second shot? Has something sparked here?

People evaluate churches in much the same way. I've heard people say, "I can't come back to your church; it's too intense." In fact, the woman I mentioned earlier told me, "I'm not coming back because I might get changed here. I was just looking for a church. I don't want a church to change my life." Isn't that sad? Essentially this person was saying, "I just want to observe someone else's date. I don't want to actually date anyone."

We need to be sensitive to negative evaluations and at the same time realize that they aren't always the end of the story. In my own life, I didn't really find the church until I was ready to leave it. It was when I didn't want to hear about God anymore that I really heard from God. Sometimes it's the pain and brokenness of our lives that finally wake us up.

> *We need to be sensitive to negative evaluations and at the same time realize that they aren't always the end of the story.*

Passion Point

Church, how are you dating the world? Are you inviting people to a fine dinner? Will you go to their homes? Will you eat their food? Will you be accompanied by Jesus? Will people experience his love, his joy, and his peace? What emotions do people experience when they are near you?

Good Manners

As a church, do we conduct ourselves well on a date? If we're going to

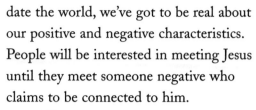

Passion Point

Does your church accept people where they are in its events, teaching, and worship? Does it consistently tell everyone, "There is a Jesus who loves you"? Is it a joyful place? Is it a place of peace and contentment?

date the world, we've got to be real about our positive and negative characteristics. People will be interested in meeting Jesus until they meet someone negative who claims to be connected to him.

Have you ever met someone you genuinely liked and then met the person's spouse and found him or her to be unlikable? You ask, "How can this be? These two don't fit or complete each other at all." As his bride, we ought to reflect our Groom's qualities. When people meet us, they should also be meeting the Groom.

We try to evaluate our manners at Hillvue. Are we kind? Do we open the door for people? Are we respectful? Do we play good music? Do we talk gently to people? Are we faithful? Do we do what we say we are going to do? Do we invite people on a date with Jesus and, when they accept, embrace them? Are we self-controlled?

We're constantly asking the folks in our congregation, "What happened today? How was church today? What did you hear today? What did you see today? What did you feel today? What did you learn? Where did you meet Jesus?" Be prepared for surprising answers, especially to the last question, because Jesus is not just in the auditorium; he's everywhere. During one of our worship services, a guy felt the Holy Spirit moving him. He felt he just had to get away for a moment so he went to the bathroom. As funny as this sounds, a connection with Jesus took place right there in the bathroom.

The Journey

Dating is a journey. It's following Jesus' voice even though we don't always know where we're going. When Jesus asks people out, he says,

"Come, follow me." Those who accept that invitation don't know where they are going; he just says, "Follow me." As they follow Jesus, they experience many things. The teaching moments occur as they evaluate the experiences. As followers of Jesus embrace these experiences, they are reshaped. This is the rhythm of dating.

Dating is a journey. It's following Jesus' voice even though we don't always know where we're going.

Hand-Holding

I remember going out on dates when I was young and trying to hold a girl's hand. During a movie, I'd place my hand on the armrest in the hope that she might touch my hand in response. The first time a young woman held my hand, I was overwhelmed by the power of that connection.

This is what the church should be doing: inviting people to extend their hands toward God. Warning—I've found that when I extend a hand toward God he will take hold of it.

Warning—I've found that when I extend a hand toward God he will take hold of it.

Desire for Further Intimacy

Dating ultimately leads to intimacy and the desire to be connected. Remember that Jesus wants to be in a marriage with us, which is the only context in which true intimacy is possible. Some people are tempted to just date and never move into intimacy. When Jesus takes hold of us, holding our hands will never be enough for him. Holding hands leads to deeper connection. In our dating, we need to constantly have marriage in mind. We want people to make the ultimate commitment to Jesus—giving him their hearts and lives.

Passion Point

Let's look at ministry in a different way. What if our ministries were preparing for a date? Instead of just planning worship, why don't we prepare for people to allow Jesus to go out with them? Think of that image. Think of how leadership will be energized by preparing a date with Jesus.

Happy Memories

On a good date, every element is memorable. In a powerful worship experience, everything should be connected to create lasting memories. The lights, the screen, the pipe organ, the liturgy, the colors, the guitar, the Communion, the invitation, the parking lot, the sounds, and the smells should all work together to create lasting memories in the hearts of people.

Getting Ready to Date

Is your church planning a date with Jesus? If so, how would that planning unfold? For example, Jesus is calling us to develop a new worship experience in our church. The first question we must ask is, Is Jesus planning the date, or are we planning the date and leaving Jesus out of the experience? If we answer that, yes, Jesus wants us to connect with the world through these plans, we may need to change the sound of our music. We may need to change our way of approaching people. We may need to change some of our expressions. What's Jesus asking us to change so that people can make a Jesus connection?

We must prepare to date Jesus. We must be constantly encountering Jesus, conversing with Jesus, having dinner with Jesus, and being reminded of who Jesus is. As we do that, we're preparing connection moments with Christ instead of just planning worship. Bible teaching is no longer just shared moments of intellectual and historical information; it's the stories of a Jesus who is connected to you and is connecting with others.

We'd better wake up in the church. The first date is always the most important one. Many times we forget that the world is always watching—not occasionally watching, but *always* watching. One bad date could mean that a long time will pass before someone goes out again. If we reject those who begin to consider Jesus, it could take a long time before they consider him again. They may *never* consider him again.

We'd better wake up in the church. The first date is always the most important one.

My friend Dick Slevin came to our church as a fifty-seven-year-old, self-confessed atheist. I met him in the lobby with a welcoming smile.

I said, "Hey, it's good to have you here."

He said, "I don't believe any of this crap. I'm here because my wife likes me to come with her. I don't even listen to you."

"Well, that's great. You're welcome to come here, sit where you want to sit, do what you need to do. Just let us know what you need."

"I'm never going to believe this stuff."

You know what? He continued to come back Sunday after Sunday. My wife considers it a challenge to make depressed or grumpy people smile or laugh. She continued to ask Dick about his life and found that he is an exceptional artist. She asked him to consider teaching painting and telling his story on canvas. He responded, "That's not a good idea."

Passion Point

I cannot overemphasize how important it is to date with passion. I'm not talking about volume; I'm talking about intensity. How intense is your dating life? Are you there to discover? Are you there to communicate? Are you there to convince?

Although he disapproved, Dick's wife eventually put a notice up on the church bulletin board advertising that he could teach painting. After one week, he didn't receive any calls. He called my wife and reminded her that he had said it wasn't a good idea.

On Easter Sunday morning two years later in a large coliseum, he left the back stands. His wife thought he had gone to smoke a cigarette, but then she saw him kneeling at the altar. He had come forward, dropped to his knees, and said to the pastors, "It is real. He is God. I have received him. *I am changed.*"

If you go out long enough, you'll really get to know somebody. If people hang around Jesus long enough, they might eventually embrace him.

Wedding Checklist

1. How is evangelism like or unlike matchmaking?

2. What are the three primary "inviting" events of your church? How effective have they been?

3. How is your church surprising people on a regular basis?

4. How does your church draw people into intimacy with God?

5. What things need to change in your church in order to help "daters" connect with Jesus?

Engaging:

Where Passionate Faith Commits

If you date someone long enough, people start asking questions. Where's your relationship going? Does he love you? Do you love him? Do you think you'll get married? You sure have been dating a long time. Has he popped the question? Do you think he will?

In all our activity as the bride, we need to constantly encourage people to consider a commitment to Jesus. Jesus is married to his bride. Nothing less than marital commitment will please him.

From "Around" to "In"

We're not in the business of just calling people to be *around* Jesus. Jesus always drew a crowd, but his mission went much further than drawing a crowd. His mission was engagement; his goal was commitment.

Churches often believe that large crowds show that the ministry is successful. Be careful of this thinking; don't be deceived. I'm not saying that we should not expose the gospel to large crowds and to everybody in our path. I am only warning that we must not just bring people *around* the gospel. Eventually, they need to be *in* the gospel.

We must not just bring people around *the gospel. Eventually, they need to be* in *the gospel.*

When we're out in the world, we're bringing people around Jesus to create the possibility of connection. Jesus went into the world and drew crowds to him to offer that possibility. Jesus fed the five thousand. Surrounded by many, he taught in parables. He performed miracles, and many people observed them.

But Jesus taught the disciples how to be *in*, not just *around*. Jesus' explanation to Nicodemus about the need to be born again was more than an "around" encounter; it was an "in" encounter. He told Nicodemus that he must be born again, or born from above. Jesus said he must enter *into* the kingdom of God, not just be *around* the kingdom of God (John 3).

Isn't that what it means to be engaged—to move from being *around* each other to being *committed* to each other? The decision to become engaged stems from a desire to be *connected* to each other.

Evaluate your own ministry. How many people in your church are content to be *around* the gospel? People like to be around people who are intriguing, accepting, loving, and kind, and we should be all these things to the world. But there's more to it. George Barna says that the American church has the knack of being around truth without necessarily being engaged in the truth.[1]

We are called to do more than love one another politely. We are called to actually engage in the struggles of other people while we urge them to engage in Christ's truth. We are called to invite and expose people to the fabulous realization that they, too, can be *in Christ.*

Popping the Question

Will you marry me? That's the question. In a real sense, that's Jesus' question as well. After you've seen Jesus, heard Jesus, and watched Jesus, you must ask yourself if you're willing to become a part of the mission. Will you enter *in?* Will you say yes?

It takes more than living according to Jesus' teaching, more than being models, to sufficiently expose others to Jesus. We are open, free, and accepted because we have said yes to Jesus. We've become a part of the bride. We have the privilege of popping the question. *Will you allow Jesus Christ to enter into you? Will you allow Jesus Christ to take you on a journey?*

If we're not popping the question, we're not taking Jesus' love for people seriously enough.

Letting Go

My wife and I were high school sweethearts. We went to college together, and then I decided that we needed to be married.

At the ripe, mature age of twenty, I thought I knew something about marriage. When I asked Elizabeth to marry me, I thought, "What's the big deal? We've been hanging around since we were fourteen or so. Surely I know this person."

Before we got engaged, I would introduce her by saying, "This is Elizabeth. She's my girlfriend. We've been dating off and on since we were in high school." After she said yes to "the big question," I began to introduce her as my fiancée. What a difference! This was serious, and our relationship was on its way to a commitment, a covenant.

I had no idea how much the covenant of marriage would change our relationship. I had no idea how deeply marriage would revolutionize my existence.

I'm not sure we understand just how deep Jesus wants to go with us. The church needs to be reminded that *Jesus is after our lives.* He's after our innermost identities. He knows all about us. He wants to engage us all in a full and abundant life. He said, "I have not come like the thief who steals and kills and destroys; I have come that they might have full and abundant life" (John 10:10, paraphrased). This key verse exposes us to the nature and intensity of the gospel of Jesus Christ. Jesus has come to connect us to a full life. He has come to engage us in a different experience. And we need to understand that *we cannot get to where Jesus wants us to be without him.*

Jesus has come to connect us to a full life. He has come to engage us in a different experience.

You must let go to get into that experience. I had to let go of my concepts of dating to begin to experience engagement. Engagement changed my relationship with others. A high school buddy couldn't understand the engagement relationship even though he had been around both Elizabeth and me for many years. He would always be a close friend to me, but our relationship would not be the same because my wife-to-be was (and is) my best friend.

Jesus is asking us to let go of our sin. He is asking us, "What are you holding on to?"

Many young men have come into my office and said, "Pastor, I'm thinking about getting married, but I'm not sure I'm ready yet. How will I know when I'm ready?"

I usually respond, "Can you let go yet?"

"What do you mean, 'let go'?"

"Can you let go of your single life to engage *in* life with another person? What about your single life are you unwilling to let go of?"

"Well, if I get married, will I still get to play golf?"

"Yes."

"If I get married, will my wife tell me what to do all the time?"

"No."

"What will being married be like?"

"I don't know," I say. "Everyone is different, but here are some things I do know. You must surrender to know your bride, and your bride must surrender to know you. We all have to let go of our *own* concepts and allow the relationship of marriage to introduce new ones. But you've got to let go of the old ones."

Becoming engaged to Jesus means letting go of our lives as we know them. Churches need to communicate this "letting go" aspect of faith, because it's Jesus' ardent desire. He wants all of us. No holds barred.

A Deeper Commitment

I often tease my congregation by saying that we could get away with some things if Jesus weren't in us. For example, a short time after one of my friends connected with Christ, he came to me and said, "I went out and tried to party with my old buddies last night, but I didn't want to. Everything was terrible; it wasn't fun anymore."

Our old behaviors are just not fun when Jesus is in us.

Becoming engaged changed the way I looked at my other relationships. It changed the way I reacted when I was tempted to flirt with others. When I was dating, I would flirt when I felt like it. But when I became engaged, I was committed. I was headed toward a covenant. *I was taken.* Flirting wasn't fun anymore.

On March 10, 1991, Hillvue Heights Church became engaged to

Jesus. The first service was more than scary. There were only a few people there, but they were willing to become engaged *in* the gospel rather than merely hearing the gospel.

As I talked with the people at Hillvue, many of them shared their dreams of what the church might be. When I asked them how long they had been talking about these possibilities, I found that God had been exposing them to the dream of a fervent church for three or four years. They had been flirting with the possibility that they could become a church that engaged their community. Then God used me as the one who would say, "You've talked about what an alive church looks like. You've seen that this church is coming back to life. Now, are you willing to allow God to engage you?"

You've talked about what an alive church looks like. You've seen that this church is coming back to life. Now, are you willing to allow God to engage you?

Who's Holding Who?

Engagement isn't us taking hold of God. God takes hold of us, and we make the decision to hold on. I'm a water-skier. Holding on is an important concept in water-skiing. The boat holds the power. The rope holds the connection. When a 310-horsepower motor pulls you out of the water, you are not taking hold of *it; it's* taking hold of *you,* and you have to decide whether to hold on.

When a 310-horsepower motor pulls you out of the water, you are not taking hold of it; it's taking hold of you, and you have to decide whether to hold on.

The church cannot tell God what to be, how to be, or what to do. We simply have the privilege of allowing God to take hold of us and holding on.

Throwing It Down

Before you put an engagement ring on someone's hand, you may need to evaluate what you hold in your hand and what you're willing to give up for the hand you'll hold.

Before God could send Moses, he asked him, "What do you hold in your hand?" Then God said, "Throw it down, Moses." Many times, as I've pastored Hillvue Heights Church, the Lord Jesus Christ has looked at me and directly, clearly, and understandably said, "Throw it down, Ayers. Throw it down, Stephen. Throw it down, pastor. Throw it down."

I don't know the exact details of Moses' response, but I sure know what my response is when God asks me to throw it down and engage in him. "But, but, but, Lord, you don't understand. If we throw this down, some people might get out of control." I remember when the Spirit began to blow through the corridors of our church. I was excited and scared at the same time, thinking, What if this gets out of control? What if *I* can't get this back?

Passion Point

Are the ministries in which you are presently engaged calling people to commit to Jesus, or are they calling people to commit to church activities? What are we engaged to? What are we engaged in? These are important questions as we evaluate the church. Are we the bride who calls people to be engaged to Jesus?

Then it dawned on me. If I'm controlling my marriage, Elizabeth and I are in big trouble. If I'm controlling the church, the church is in *really* big trouble. The engagement shapes us; we don't shape the engagement. The engagement is all about Jesus. It's *his* truth, forgiveness, love, and power. It's not even about our ability to hold on; it's about Jesus' ability to take hold of us.

Church, now's the time to awaken as pastors, praise and worship leaders, faith developers, Christian educators, gospel evangelists, priests, rectors, and connectors of a great loving God to the world. But we've got to throw it down.

Pastoring a church has meant that I've had to throw down several things.

First, *I had to throw down my own ideas about church.*

Second, *I had to throw down my ideas of what a successful pastor is.* In fact, before I could lead a Spirit-journeying church, I had to let go of my own journey. There's a career path in the denomination in which I serve, and then there's Jesus' path. The career path is to use a 250- or 300-member church as a steppingstone to the next larger church. But Jesus said, "Go to a thirty-member church—a broken-down, busted, without-any-glimpse-of-human-hope church—step in there, and I'll show you that *I* am God."

Third, *I had to throw down my ego, my ambition, and my drive in order to receive* his *drive.*

This is engagement, and in no way would I suggest to you that it's easy. It was so difficult for me. I believe that Moses said, "Lord, but, but, but you don't understand. This is a rod. This is *my* rod. This is *my* security. This is *my* friend. This is *my* image."

Have you ever noticed that God never changes his mind?

"Throw it down, Moses."

When we engage with God, we might expect to enter a beautiful, peaceful state in which all our stress is relieved and everybody becomes polite and wonderful. We might expect God to ask us to throw down something that is easy to throw down. But these are not the episodes described in the gospel.

When Moses threw the rod on the ground, it turned into a snake. And it wasn't just a snake; it was a hissing snake that could bite. Church, as we engage the world and call it to commit to Jesus Christ, we will have the same kind of experience. The more accepting, loving, and open I become, the more hits and insults I take. But I also understand grace more and more. How can it be that God loves us, even when we're unacceptable? God stays engaged with us, even when we want to disengage. This is the hope of glory that is not *around* you but *in* you because you've received Jesus.

Many times people have come into my office and said, "I received Jesus, but this week has been a nightmare." They then described weeks full of hissing snakes. Sometimes when we make the decision to receive Jesus, there's a hissing snake awaiting us. Then comes the moment we're asked to trust. For Moses, it was God's command to pick the snake up by the tail. Logic, reason, and experience advised against doing that. But in ministry, logic, reason, and experience aren't always the greatest evaluation tools.

In ministry, logic, reason, and experience aren't always the greatest evaluation tools.

"Pick it up by the tail, Moses."

I grew up in Kentucky; I've definitely seen some rattlesnakes and copperheads. I don't like snakes, and I don't like things to be out of my control. I say chop off the head of a hissing snake. I want to face the situation in my own way, and then I hear God calling me, and I remember that…God made the snake.

"Pick it up, Moses." Pick it up, church. Pick it up by the tail. When we think about calling this world to engage in Jesus Christ, the metaphor of the hissing snake becomes a reality for all of us. Most of us, when we see hissing snakes, do as I do. We run!

You can probably think of many illustrations of this point. There are hissing snakes for every one of us to pick up. The engagement with Jesus occurs when we're willing to pick up what he's offering. Jesus calls us to surrender our lives, philosophies, experiences, and ideas. He calls us to throw them down, and, even if they turn into hissing snakes, to pick up what he gives us.

The first engagement battle in our church was over praise and worship. For the first two years of our engagement, our church had the typical organ and piano, and we sang a few hymns. Our church began to grow and move because we were committed to saying, "Jesus Christ will change your life." God was taking hold of us during this time. As people's lives were being changed, praise and worship in our church became a way to express what was going on *inside* people.

One man in the church said, "I'm going to leave the church. I don't like this direction. I don't like all of this celebration. I don't like this praise." A leader in the church, he went behind my back and behind the backs of other church leaders and began to plan my removal from the church.

In the process of organizing his coup, he came to a meeting of deacon elders. I thought, "Here we go." I was ready to pack my bags. I was ready to say, "Well, it worked for a little while."

The man did something that I've seen other so-called leaders do. He said that he had been praying and that he and his wife felt led to leave the church. Translation: He wanted the deacon elders to beg him to stay.

I was watching carefully, and I knew the Spirit of God had to be present because I actually remained silent. I watched as one of the deacon elders stood up and said, "You know, I appreciate that you and your wife have prayed. In fact, I'm in agreement that your prayer was of God and that God has called you to leave this church. I want us as deacon elders to pray over you and your family, that you will find a congregation that is of your particular expression and that you advance the kingdom of God."

I could not get out of my chair. I blessed the brother from a distance because I couldn't even move. I was shocked. I was amazed. These leaders, after two years, had become engaged in the purpose of the gospel, and they knew that this purpose was greater than their individual worship preferences.

I know a husband and wife who had two children and then later divorced. The woman began attending Hillvue, found Jesus, and then invited her ex-husband to come and experience the same Jesus. When they found Christ, when they knew their sins were forgiven, when they understood that a new, changed life had entered into them—guess what happened. Two years later, they picked up a marriage that had been disastrous, threw down all the disastrous parts, and picked up a new marriage in Jesus Christ. They've celebrated this marriage for eight years now. When you see experiences like this, you know that engaging in the gospel and being *in* the gospel are different from being *around* the gospel.

One of my buddies picked up a relationship with his wife even though she had been involved in an affair. In Christ, he picked that covenant back up and found that the marriage that had ended in infidelity was a marriage that could be lived in Christ Jesus' fidelity. A marriage that had been plundered was now being driven by Christ's permanent connection to him. Picking up the hissing snake means we're to be a part of Christ in such a significant way that we show the world that being engaged with Jesus is the best way to live.

Passion Point

Consider your own ministry. What needs to be thrown down? What in your life is a hissing snake? What needs to be picked up? Warning—do not pick it up unless God tells you to pick it up. I don't know about your pastorate, but I know about mine. There are a lot of hissing snakes in my church, a lot of negative comments, and a lot of people who want to tell me what I need to do. I imagine I'm not alone.

We need to be *permanently* committed to the truth that Jesus is in charge. When Jesus is in charge and tells us to pick up a hissing snake, we can be convinced that picking up that hissing snake is the right thing to do. When Jesus takes hold of us, when we become engaged, when we become involved in the love and joy of Christ, the church begins to flourish.

This is what it takes to be engaged with God. No longer is it our expression that is important; it's God's expression within us that becomes essential. I encourage you to throw down whatever God asks you to throw down and to then pick up whatever God asks you to pick up—even if it's turned into a hissing snake. We are to *receive* the power of God; we can't *create* it. When you can pick up a snake, you can face Pharaoh with confidence. When you come to a dead end in your ministry, when the Red Sea is in front of you and the attacking army is closing in behind you, you can look to God on high, a God who is in charge, and say, "Lord, if you don't do something, nothing's going to happen." As you lift up the rod that used to be a hissing snake, the waters will part, and you can walk across.

Permanent Engagement

Jesus won't go away. That is the beautiful, historical promise of the past two thousand years. *Jesus will not go away.* The love of God is permanent for those who have received him.

As you read this, you might be thinking, "Well, it's just so hard to talk about a permanent relationship in such a temporary culture." I argue that the opposite is true. Permanent relationships have become a mystery in the midst of a temporary, self-indulgent culture. Your church can become a place where the mystery is revealed. The world asks how our people hold on when it gets tough. When we become engaged, we're actually making a promise to hang in there with one another, stay with one another, and journey with one another. Through Jesus Christ, God is always with us. "Just as you received Christ Jesus as Lord, continue to live in him, rooted and built up in him, strengthened in the faith as you were taught, and overflowing with thankfulness" (Colossians 2:6-7).

We're also warned in verse 8, "See to it that no one takes you captive through hollow and deceptive philosophy, which depends on human tradition and the basic principles of this world rather than on Christ." The world emphasizes temporary relationships, while God tells us that our relationship with him is permanent when we become willing to engage. We become engaged when we distinctly and definitely say, "I will follow you, Jesus. I will follow you wherever you go."

When we were juniors in high school, Elizabeth and I were in a business-law class together. I made some smart-aleck, chauvinistic comment, and she abruptly stood up and said, "Only a fool would marry you anyway, Steve Ayers." Of course, the class—and our teacher—agreed with her.

Several years later, when I asked her to marry me, I laid out the possibility of our life together. I told her that I'd preach fervently. I told her that God had given me all kinds of wild and crazy ideas about his church, so we'd probably be fired every two years. We'd probably live all over America. We'd probably *never* have stability. We'd probably know lots of people who didn't like us and a few who did. We'd enjoy God. We'd be together in the whole deal. We wouldn't have much money. And we'd be in the ministry.

Then I paused, remembering her comment in that business-law class, and said, "Hey, I want to ask you a question tonight."

"What?"

"Would you like to be the fool?"

When I said that, I pulled out the ring. Crying and laughing at the same time, she said, "I'll be the fool." I'm so glad she was willing to be the fool, because she has brought a deeper understanding of Christ into my life. None of it's foolish. It was Paul who said the foolish things of Christ would baffle the wisdom of the world. Where are the churches that truly believe this?

"Would you like to be the fool?"

Many in our culture may think that marriage, engagement, and permanent commitment are old-fashioned, foolish ideas. I encourage the church to hold on to the biblical text. Allow the mystery of its stories to engage the culture.

My engagement with Christ is a mystery to those who don't know him. They ask, "Why Jesus? Why do you follow Jesus?"

I respond, "Because I've found forgiveness in Christ. I've found love in Christ. I've found acceptance in Christ." Then I usually finish the answer with this mysterious statement: "And I'm just fool enough to believe it's true." This statement unlocks the door to fervent churches. Our churches need to become foolish enough to believe it will work. We've got to hold on and not be ashamed of the gospel.

Think about your own life. Think about your church. Think about your family. Think about how God truly does engage us. The world is waiting to see if our faith *works*. Lots of people wondered if Elizabeth and I would stay together. Many still marvel that Elizabeth has stayed with such a spontaneous, on-the-go guy. I'm full of passion and surprise. My wife is full of grace and stability. We both have fallen in love with Jesus, and that's what enables our marriage to thrive.

Engagement Parties

Engagement calls for celebration. We've learned to celebrate engagement at Hillvue Heights Church. I encourage all of us in our churches to develop ways to celebrate God's promise to us. The occasion may be a confirmation class; it may be another public declaration of faith. In our particular tradition, baptism is an act celebrating a believer's engagement to God. We use immersion baptism, symbolizing that our old selves have been buried in Christ. The old stuff is gone; we've thrown it down; we're willing to give it up. When we come up out of the water, we're welcomed to a new life in Jesus Christ.

Is your church celebrating the choice to become engaged to Jesus Christ? Is it celebrating the people who have decided to be foolish enough to receive Christ Jesus as their Lord and trust him to give them a new life? It's time that churches throw parties for people who are willing to engage with Jesus. We live in a party culture, but the church hasn't done a good job of throwing the ultimate party.

We live in a party culture, but the church hasn't done a good job of throwing the ultimate party.

Do you remember the prodigal son? It's that motif that drives our church. At Hillvue we pastor the church of the prodigals—those who had a sense of God at one time, those who were *around* God at one time, those who flirted with the possibilities of God, and those who grew up in the church but eventually went their own way. The prodigal went his own way. He spent his life on frivolous things. That is the story of American culture. How many frivolous things have we spent our lives doing? Jesus is calling us to spend our lives with him.

Remember what happened when the prodigal son returned? The father ran down the road, hugged him, and kissed him. He gave his son a new ring, new shoes, new robe, and a new life. Then he threw a party. I encourage you, as you celebrate being a bride, being connected to Jesus, and having a changed life, to *throw parties!*

Now, let me warn you. Religious people don't like parties; they like structures. Religious people don't like celebrations; they like protocol. The self-righteous brother resented the celebration for his brother, the prodigal. The Reformation revealed many truths about God, but as we reformed things of the church, we made them just a little too plain. Look around; God loves color. Awaken yourself to the morning sky, and see God's artistry. God loves color. God is expressive. And I believe that God is the Lord of the party.

Some people feel the Spirit of God in our church from the moment they step out of their cars in the parking lot. Why? People are saying yes to God. When they do that, celebration breaks out. Commitment to God naturally gives rise to celebration. Celebration *does not* create commitment. I'm not talking about celebration for celebration's sake; I'm talking about celebration because people have committed their lives to the living God. If this isn't cause for celebration, what is?

God's love changes lives. Being engaged to God begins with learning that Jesus loves us. The possibility that this truth may be too simple for complex and sophisticated minds doesn't change the revolutionary truth of Jesus. He loves us. He wants to be in us, and when we receive Jesus, it's Jesus who takes hold of us. When he does, we can no longer be the same.

Expressions of Love

Passion Point

What does your church love

so much that it can't live

without it? Is it the church's

style or structure? Is it the

way it presents itself? Is it

the people? Or does your

church love Jesus so much

that it is compelled to engage

the world?

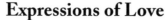

Engaging people in the message of Christ begins with love. Jesus loved us first; now we can love the world. *My* love is not strong enough to change the world. The love of my church and the loving nature of the church I participate in are not enough to change the world. However, the love that has been placed in us through the grace of Jesus Christ has the ability, even in a culture of upheaval, to transform lives and to place people on a different plane of existence.

I'm often asked why Hillvue Heights Church attracts people. I respond, "We're learning to love God more than everything else." This is a process, and it occurs first intellectually and philosophically. We begin to realize that it's all about loving Jesus. As we love Jesus, following Jesus is a natural response. It's important that we're attractive to the world, because that attractiveness shows that we've been loved.

It's important that we're attractive to the world, because that attractiveness shows that we've been loved.

The church has the wonderful responsibility of exposing the world to the love of Christ. This is our mission. "For God so loved the world that he gave his one and only Son, that whoever believes in him shall not perish but have eternal life" (John 3:16). Because we know this truth, we need to expose the world to it.

Church, we're called to be in love. We're not called to an

encumbering, miserable experience. Being in love is a committed experience. We're in love. "You look so good in love." The longer we're loved, the better we should look.

Church, maybe we've replaced the love of God with structures, methodologies, and theologies. I'm not calling the existence of all those aspects of pastoring a church into question, but I'm asking if they help people understand that they're loved by God. Or do these systems merely help us feed the organization?

You can evaluate the love factor in your church by listening to the stories of the people in your church. As pastors, we should be constantly listening. One of the greatest tools of love is not our voice but our ears. We need to listen to God to know we are loved. We also need to listen to the people to see if the story of the love and nature of God is being told to the world.

Think of the disciple Peter. He hung around Jesus. He attempted to understand Jesus; sometimes he got it right, and sometimes he failed miserably. If we honestly evaluate our own journeys, we'll realize that we've had it right at times and we've failed miserably at others. Jesus loved Peter when he failed and when he succeeded. Jesus will always love us, too.

An engagement is a promise to persevere. Jesus promises that the grace he's given us will bring us through whatever we face. It will stay with us in all seasons. The glory of God will be revealed in us. Jesus seeks not to leave us or punish us, but to embrace us and show us the truth. The Gospel of John ends with Jesus' reinstatement of his disciple Peter.

To ask the world to fall in love with Jesus, we must understand that God is in love with us. Sometimes pastors can be very lonely. We talk about

> *Passion Point*
>
> *Church, do we want to be with Jesus? Do we want to be married to him? Will we say yes to his proposal and allow him to create new life within us?*

grace. We teach about love. We ponder and explore how far God will carry his church. We see dreams and visions. In the midst of dreaming dreams, having visions, leading churches, being involved in worship services and conferences, and letting the world know that Jesus is Lord, we can forget the most important thing: Jesus loves us.

You're not just a preacher, praise and worship leader, children's pastor, youth worker, or church member; you are a part of Christ, and he loves you. Pastor, know that you're loved by God and that when others in the church don't love you, you're loved by the head of the church—Jesus himself. Sometimes in the ministry, it's all we have left—"Jesus loves me." Isn't it wonderful to know that when all else fails, "Jesus loves me" is enough?

I don't need my territory expanded; I just need to make the most of the territory I've already been given. Jesus' love is enough to bring me through all eternity. God himself, who became one of us, loves me to the point that he wants me to go and share his love with others. Being loved by God and loving God is what enables us to engage others and encourage them to become engaged to Jesus Christ.

I don't need my territory expanded; I just need to make the most of the territory I've already been given.

But I will not experience the fullness of God's love as long as I hold on to things that I love more than I love him. For a long time, I struggled because I loved material things more than I loved Jesus. I didn't enter into the ministry with an open heart and a wonderful vision. Instead I asked, "Lord, why me? Let me be a good deacon. Let me be a great businessperson. Let me coach football. Please, Lord, why the church?" Twenty years later, I realize that it's because the church is his bride and he loves the church. Even when she's fickle and haughty, thinks she's running the show, and won't do what he calls her to do, she is bathed in Jesus' love, which she cannot control.

Take a personal inventory. What in the church do you love more than Jesus? Good things are not as great as Jesus. You can have good music, but if it doesn't stem from a love of Jesus, it's not great music. You can have good preaching, but if it's not based on a love of Jesus, it will never be great preaching. You can have a warm, inviting, positive fellowship that seeks to welcome people in polite, positive ways, but if it doesn't love Jesus above all, it will never be great. Jesus doesn't call us to an average relationship; he calls us to an extraordinary relationship through grace.

Jesus asked Peter, "Do you love me? Do you love me more than these?"

Peter's first response was much the same as ours would be. Immediately he said, "Yes, Lord, you know I love you."

"Feed my lambs."

Church, we're in the job of connecting people. We're feeding lambs and connecting them to the Source of life. We feed lambs to show them the Shepherd. Feed lambs. Feed people on the love given to you. Jesus asked and commanded, "Do you love me? Then take care of my sheep."

The love of God will be illustrated to the world by the way we take care of the sheep. One of the ways we take care of the sheep is by telling them the truth. Jesus loves them. Jesus wants to be with them. Jesus will change things. Even if it's difficult, Jesus will come through. We don't back off because they disagree. We feed them.

One time I actually observed a herd of sheep, and I could see that they need shepherds. Without shepherds, sheep just do their own thing, and they miss out on the best thing.

We don't back off because they disagree. We feed them.

If we in the church don't submit to the Shepherd, guess what. We do our own thing. We fall in love with everything except Jesus. It's so easy to have an affair and betray Jesus. The things of this world are alluring. Sometimes it's so tempting to indulge in lust at the expense of love.

The power of the gospel is simple. We are called to follow Jesus wherever he may go. Follow Jesus. Follow him as Lord. Follow him as Savior. Follow him. Hillvue Heights Church has learned to simply follow Jesus.

Warning—when you connect, when you know that you are permanently connected with Christ Jesus, and when you follow him, the Lord will take you to places you thought you would never go.

I thought I would never be in an explosive church that welcomed all kinds of people. I never thought I'd be in a church where addicts became free of their addictions and marriages that had ended were knit back together, where children found new life, and where several ethnic groups came together in harmony. I never dreamed of pastoring that church. As I followed him, God's plan was revealed.

———————————————————————————————

Warning—when you connect and know that you are permanently connected with Christ Jesus, and when you follow him, the Lord will take you to places you thought you would never go.

———————————————————————————————

Together Through It All

I've known couples who have been married for well over fifty years. They've endured hard times, enjoyed good times, and decided to love each other relentlessly no matter what. Over time they began to think each other's thoughts and look like a matched pair. The bride began to look more like the groom. When we say yes to the Lord and go wherever he takes us, the church will more and more resemble Jesus, reflecting his love and his grace to a world hungry for both.

Wedding Checklist

1. How important are large crowds to your church? Have you become satisfied with merely getting people *around* the gospel without getting them *in* the gospel?

2. What are the "deeper level" ministries in your church? What are some new ministries you could add to move people into greater degrees of commitment?

3. Get members of your staff together, and ask them to wrestle with this question: How is your area of ministry reaching new people and, at the same time, leading the regulars into deeper levels of commitment?

4. How is your church helping people celebrate new levels of commitment in their lives? Perhaps you need to think about forming a "party ministry."

5. What are some creative ways that your church could communicate the fact that Jesus is its greatest love?

Marrying:
Where Passionate Faith Triumphs

Engagement finally culminates in the big day—the wedding day—the day love triumphs. Nothing compares with a love that enters into the bond of a covenant commitment. Without a doubt, it's the high point of human love.

In the church, we ask people, "Would you like to follow Jesus? Would you like Jesus to come into your life?" Spiritual marriage happens when they say, "Yes, I'll follow Jesus Christ. I'll believe in his cross and his resurrection. I'll receive his forgiveness." The church's mission is to get people to this point—connecting with God through Jesus Christ. It's helping people enter into a passionate, spiritual marriage covenant with God's Son. What a mission! What a purpose! Church, it's time for us to wake the people of this world up to the fact that Jesus Christ truly wants to be married to them. He wants them to be a part of his bride.

What Is Marriage, Really?

What does it mean to be married? For one thing, it's scary. I've never led a wedding service in which the groom and the bride weren't nervous. Knees knock; hands shake. But marital fear isn't bad. It's simply the overwhelming realization that our lives will change because we're giving them to someone else. In spiritual marriage, our lives change as surely as they do in physical marriage. Galatians 2:20 tells us that we've been crucified with Christ and now we're risen in Christ. The people we were have morphed into new creations.

We're changed because of Jesus' love for us. We're his *bride*. We're his *treasure*. We're his *church*. We're his instruments of peace. We're his *voice*. We're his *revelation*. We're the *reality* of the *gospel*.

We're his bride. *We're his* treasure. *We're his* church. *We're his* instruments of peace. *We're his* voice. *We're his* revelation. *We're the* reality *of the* gospel.

Spiritual marriage occurs when we confess our faith in Jesus, telling the world that he is our Lord. When Jesus asked us to believe in him, we said, "Yes, we will." When Jesus asked if we believed our sins could be forgiven in him, we said, "Yes, we do." Eventually, we proclaimed, "We are with Jesus." That was the day that everything changed. That was the day we connected with Jesus.

The power of evangelism starts with your own understanding of your connection with Christ. When I first started sharing the faith, I was merely sharing the *story* of the faith. A little further along in my Christian walk, I began to share the *results* of the story of Christ. Now I have begun to understand that I am a *part* of the story of Christ. I am connected to his eternity. I'm married into a covenant with Jesus. What a cause for celebration!

At Hillvue, there are two events we always celebrate. We always celebrate when people acknowledge their need to be changed by Jesus. We still have an altar call. We still ask people to come forward and receive Jesus Christ. When they ask Jesus Christ into their lives, we cheer, clap, hug, welcome them, and celebrate the fact that they've received the grace of God.

We always celebrate baptism. Our particular tradition practices immersion baptism. As we were building a new worship center, we debated where to put the baptistry. At first we planned to put it over to the side of the stage. However, one of the deacon elders spoke up: "You know, this is one of the

Passion Point

What is your particular community of faith doing to celebrate the intimacy of this relationship? As a pastor, do you just go through the week—hoping to get through another sermon; hoping to make it through another counseling appointment; hoping that someday, somehow, all of this activity will make sense? Or do you wake up and say, "This is the day the Lord has made. I'm going to be glad, and I'm going to rejoice in it, because I know Jesus is with me. Because of that, I can now go and share with the nations what it means to be a disciple of Christ, what it means to be the bride of a holy God"?

most important celebrations in our community of faith. I think the baptistry should be in the middle of the stage and lifted up so everybody can see our celebration of the beginning of a new life."

After that declaration, we all conceded that the baptistry should be lifted up, not to lift up baptism, but to intensify the celebration. Notice I said *celebration*, not *ceremony*. Entering into new life in Jesus is worthy of joyous celebration.

Celebrating New Life

It's important that the church truly celebrate spiritual marriages. I've been to churches in which people who have made a faith commitment to Jesus were greeted with something like, "OK, yeah, well, that's nice. That's good. Here, fill out this card." I encourage you to consider carefully how your church celebrates decisions to follow Jesus. Is there a time of pronouncement that tells those who have decided to follow Jesus that, without a doubt, they have stepped into a new life?

Some traditions use confirmation classes to help people understand the grace that's been given to them. If your church practices confirmation, be sure to celebrate the new life that's beginning. Be sure to say, "Welcome to the journey. Welcome to the power. Welcome to the passion." How can we sit idly when we know this is the day someone has met Jesus? The celebration doesn't have to be loud; it just has to be recognized. Others need to know that someone has been connected in Jesus Christ.

The celebration doesn't have to be loud; it just has to be recognized.

My friend Terry attended another church for more than ten years. During that time, he and I developed a relationship. We talked and laughed with each other. Both of us are big football fans, so we discussed our favorite teams, cheered with each other, and even cheered against each other. Then one morning Terry was at the altar.

I looked at him and said, "Terry, what's up, man?"

"Today's the day."

"What do you mean?"

"I now believe what you've been telling me for about a year and a half. I believe that Jesus did die for me. I believe that Jesus has entered into my life. I guess I'm going to be saved."

"You mean, you didn't know Jesus?"

"Well, I knew about Jesus, but nobody ever asked me if I really had him in my life. I've never had this conversion experience. But today I became convinced that Jesus is truly who he said he is. I want Jesus to come into my life, and I want my sins to be forgiven."

Terry prayed a prayer of confession and asked Jesus to forgive him of his sins. The Lord Jesus entered into his life. Two weeks later he would be baptized.

He called me on the phone the Thursday night before his baptism and said, "I'm excited, but, you know, I feel some anxiety about this."

"What is it?"

"I know that when I come out of that baptistry, I will have declared that I'm different, that I have a new life. What if I stumble? What if I fall? I remember you told me that Jesus is the one who's going to hold us up. Sunday, I'm going to trust Jesus to hold me up. I'm going to trust Jesus to give me a new life. It's about Jesus."

Terry's baptism was a celebration. On that particular morning, people broke out with cheers, praises, and thanks. Eventually, Terry saw his wife come to Jesus, along with his children and one of his best friends. He had the opportunity to baptize them, with one of our pastors, as he was the one who had pointed them to their connection with Christ.

I said, "Terry, what caused them to want to connect to Christ?"

"They don't want to miss the celebration. They want to have the same joy I have."

I encourage you not to fear open celebration or declaring to the world your love for Jesus. We hide nothing at our church. We don't hide the Holy Spirit. We don't hide praise. We don't hide worship. We have crosses in our auditorium. We tell you straight up that we believe that Jesus Christ is the way, the truth, and the life. We welcome you to be intimately connected to Jesus. Some would ask, "Are some people offended?" Well, yes, some are, but many more begin to consider that this Jesus could be real. And many of them will connect themselves to the grace of Jesus Christ.

Many of us will be surprised to find out that Jesus isn't half as stoic and toned-down as religion makes him out to be. Jesus dances, connects, and welcomes the unwelcome. His bride ought to reflect his image.

Many of us will be surprised to find out that Jesus isn't half as stoic and toned-down as religion makes him out to be. Jesus dances, connects, and welcomes the unwelcome. His bride ought to reflect his image.

The Significance of Marriage

What is a wedding ceremony? It's a celebration of the covenant between two people who have fallen in love. The celebration includes vows, confession, perhaps a unity candle, and Holy Communion. We use the opportunity to say, "God, thank you for the love you've given us for each other. Please connect us and bless us." The two shall become one.

Passion Point

I encourage you to think about your own congregation right now. It's even more important that you think about your own life. How long has it been since you, as a church leader, went out with someone and shared the story of Jesus' grace? What kind of story is unfolding in your own spiritual journey right now? Is it a story about the mechanics or process of the church, or is it a story about an intimate relationship with Jesus? Do you understand that you, as a church leader, are not just a conductor of the ceremony? You stand in the position of the bride.

Believers become one with Christ. This doesn't mean we lose our identity. Rather we find our identity in Jesus Christ. We find out who we really are. We really are designed to be with God. Reflect on that for just a moment. God desires to be with us. I've seen that very simple message change the lives of so many people. Did you know that Jesus just wants to be with you? He wants to love you. He wants to give you grace. He wants to give you freedom. He wants you to know the truth of his salvation and his love and his power to set you free to live as you were designed to live.

Post-Wedding Blues

After the wedding celebration, things can get tough. When they do, we begin to learn how to live out the covenant relationship we've entered. Like marriage, salvation is a journey that continues for life.

When I woke up the morning after our wedding, I was excited, tired, and amazed. I was emotionally drained. I felt joy and anxiety at the same time. When my eyes began to focus, I looked down at my finger and was amazed. I had gotten married. I couldn't believe that Elizabeth would marry someone like me. I was only twenty years old. It took me several years to truly enter into marriage.

As we help people in the church develop, we must realize that salvation is the starting point. We must be sure, especially in churches that celebrate that initial life-changing experience, not to leave it there. I tell people all the time, "A wedding will never make a marriage." A baptism will never make a disciple. We must move people toward living life in Christ. Celebration is definitely a part of how we help people connect with Jesus. The realization that Jesus Christ is intimately in love with us is crucial. Then comes the hard part—the practice of marriage.

A wedding will never make a marriage. A baptism will never make a disciple. We must move people toward living life in Christ.

Give It Up

Marriage is frustrating as well as exciting. To truly engage in marriage, I had to give up myself to learn to love the woman who loved me. She also had to give up herself to learn to love the man who loved her. As I began to journey with Jesus, I also had to learn to give myself up. This is a tough way to live, especially in American culture.

I hear this question all the time from my buddies: "Well, Ayers, if I decide to follow Christ, will I have to quit doing this or doing that? What if I did this or that as a believer in Jesus Christ?"

Here's what I say: "It's kind of like being married. When you got married, you didn't know all that was going to happen, but you entered into the marriage anyway. As you began to live out the marriage, the truth of the relationship emerged. It's the same in a relationship with Jesus."

As a church, we've also got to give up some things to live out our relationship with Jesus. Maybe we need to give up some religious traditions to find intimacy. Sometimes it's our personal perspectives that block us from the reality of God.

We have a generation coming up that's been through divorce, drug addiction, and astounding technological developments. These people are wondering if they can have authentic permanent relationships. They're wondering if there are any relationships out there that will last. Where is the church in the midst of this? Could we choose to be so radical that we live out our connection with Jesus Christ so intimately and so passionately that the world would long to share what we have?

Could we choose to be so radical that we live out our connection with Jesus Christ so intimately and so passionately that the world would long to share what we have?

The Lifestyle of Marriage

Even though the wedding will never make the marriage, people can become obsessed with weddings. They get so caught up in the *presentation* that they miss the purpose. The church has done the same thing. It's time for us as the church to evaluate what we're declaring to the world. Are we telling the world to connect in a living relationship with Jesus, or are we telling the world to come to our particular church so we can verify our successful existence by attendance numbers?

Listen carefully. The size of the wedding celebration will never determine the quality and the intimacy of the marriage. I've witnessed wedding celebrations on houseboats as well as full-blown cathedral weddings that cost many thousands of dollars. When the bride and groom walked out, they were just as married either way. It's not what we spend on the presentation that really draws people to Christ; it's how we live out our connection with Jesus that really allows the world to see if the message we proclaim is true.

If you're in a congregation of one hundred members or less, I want to lift you up in the name of Jesus. I want to thank all those pastors who illustrate a connection with Christ in sparsely populated rural areas. Your church can be just as connected, vibrant, strong, and explosive as any church in America.

Marriage Produces Unity

We're in a kingdom. That's amazing when you stop to think about it. If you're preaching Jesus crucified and resurrected as the way into the kingdom of God, if you're proclaiming the truths of Scripture, I'm on your side. You're on my side. We're in the kingdom together.

Pastors in our community were blown away when I first started sending people to their churches. One morning, a man who had recently moved to our city visited our church. Our church is highly spirited in its worship. We use a full praise and worship band, and at times the praise choruses we sing have a Lynyrd Skynyrd sound. We're a group of Southern boys and girls who have met the Lord Jesus Christ in a very passionate way. Southern rock 'n' roll illustrates some of our worship. I met our visitor in the back of the church.

He asked, "Is this a Southern Baptist church?"

"Yes, this is a Southern Baptist church, but it's not your daddy's Southern Baptist church."

He smiled. "So it's a new generation Southern Baptist church."

"I don't know if it's the new generation Southern Baptist church. If you read your history, it might be the old generation Southern Baptist church remaking itself in a new day."

"I need a church with an organ."

"Man, let me tell you about another great church. I know you're new in town. You'll love this pastor. You'll love this church."

He was amazed. "You mean, you're sending me to another church?"

"Oh, yes, sir. I want you to be where you can celebrate your connection with Jesus. You're not going to feel as connected here as you will at another Baptist church. There's a wonderful pastor at the church I'm sending you to, a pastor who's preaching Jesus and who loves the Lord. The people there are wonderful."

"How do you know that?"

"I grew up there."

"You grew up in a Southern Baptist church?"

"Yes. I fell in love with its message: Love Jesus, live Jesus, and tell the world about Jesus."

"Why do you do worship like this?"

"I didn't fall in love with the church's *expression*. I fell in love with its *connection*."

What are you in love with? What are you in love with as you do church? Has your marriage to Jesus produced true unity with the rest of the bride, in all her many forms and expressions?

Has your marriage to Jesus produced true unity with the rest of the bride, in all her many forms and expressions?

The Risk of Married Life

Marriage is a risk. The reason our knees knock, the reason our hands shake, is that our lives are going to change after we get married. Our lives change when we are wed to Jesus. When I was a child, I did childish things. When I became a grown-up, I did grown-up things. When I was unforgiven, I did unforgiven things. Now that I'm forgiven, I can do forgiveness things. We see but a poor reflection as in a mirror, but one day we shall see face to face.

This is the great rhythm of the Christian life. Every day that we meet together, every occasion we have to be with one another, the image and reflection of Jesus should become clearer. Every day that we get to walk the face of the earth, we should treasure it and continue to discover who we are in Christ, who the church is with Christ, and how others can be connected to Christ. Let's put away things that keep us from intimacy.

Marital Passion

If I could summarize the church in one word it would be *passion*. It's the passion of connection, the passion of togetherness, the passion of dreaming dreams together—that's what the church is about. If I could describe Hillvue Heights Church in one word, it would be *passion*. If I could describe salvation in one word, it would be *passion*. If I could describe marriage in one word, it would be *passion*.

What is passion? It's the response to the intimacy and reality of God moving through our lives. It's *in* us and it flows *from* us.

I've heard people say, "I don't know how I'd make it without Jesus." In the same way, I don't know how to do church without Jesus. I don't know how to find joy, peace, and love without Jesus. Has the institutional life of your church overwhelmed its passion?

Unfortunately, many of us associate passion strictly with emotion. But in truth, our passion for God should affect every area of our lives. We should worship with passion, pray with passion, and engage in the teachings of Jesus with passion. We should live and serve others with passion. We should proclaim that Jesus passionately loves people and wants to be intimately involved with them. If not for Jesus, there would be no church. Let's preach Jesus.

In spiritual marriage, just as in physical marriage, one of the greatest pitfalls is falling into a routine, the routine of everyday life, the routine of doing it the same way every time. Routine can *kill* a relationship. Falling into the routine of religious tradition or practice can cause us to forget Who is guiding the experience. Jesus wants his church to be a radiant bride. We become radiant when we're loved. We must be careful not to replace God's love with religious systems.

This is a critical issue for the church of the twenty-first century. We have a world that is crying out to us, asking us if this Jesus message really works.

One of the greatest tools of evangelism that I've discovered, especially in the last twelve years, is letting the passion of God flow, even when I don't understand it. I encourage you to let the passion of God be a part of everything you do in ministry.

I'm not talking about being loud. I'm not talking about being fast. I'm not talking about being super-polished. I am talking about being connected with the love of Christ in every practice of the church, realizing that we come to a church and are part of a church so we might fully and clearly understand our connection with Christ.

Who Do You Love?

The other day as my wife and I were traveling, we stopped at a deli for lunch. We were laughing and goofing off, as we usually do.

A woman sitting nearby looked at us and said, "You must be newlyweds."

We said, "No, we've been married for eighteen years and have dated each other most of our lives."

"And you still like marriage and each other?"

I replied, "It only gets better. We've had our problems, but it keeps getting better."

If we will live out our passion for God, people will ask us what's going on. At Pentecost, Peter was anointed with God's power as he stood and told people that Jesus crucified and resurrected is the way and the truth. His

Passion Point

When people come to your church, who and what do they hear? More than once, I've picked up a church bulletin, looked at the message, and read more about what that church is doing than what Jesus is doing with the church. The message of Jesus' forgiveness, grace, and connection should drive all we do. We need to interrupt the routine and the system of the church to evaluate who is truly being glorified.

words caused the people to ask, "What must we do to be a part of this?" (Acts 2:14-37, paraphrased).

Church, release your passion. The good news is that you don't have to take a seminar to do it. The passion is already there.

You may need to evaluate what you're in love with. Many people who are thinking about divorce say, "I've fallen out of love." These words can often be translated as "I haven't invested the time necessary to develop the relationship." The church needs to be in love with Jesus. What's your church truly in love with? I'm not asking you about its purpose or its mechanics. I'm asking you a very pointed question. What are you in love with?

My marriage was messed up at the beginning because I was more in love with money than with my wife. It stings to be that honest. The church must be just as honest. I'm not asking you if your church is growing numerically. I'm not asking you if you are serving and feeding hungry people in a thousand different ways. I'm not asking about doctrine. I'm asking the question that forces you to evaluate the state of your spiritual marriage: *What are you in love with?*

It's easy for the church to fall in love with many things other than Jesus. We must be careful to be married to Christ, his grace, and his concerns alone. If we are, the church will explode.

When we fall in love with Jesus, we'll do what he says. According to 1 John 5, those who love the child love the father, those who love God are obedient to his commandments, and God's commandments are not a burden. Isn't that interesting? When we fall in love with Jesus, what he commands us to do is no longer a burden, but a joy. What are you in love with?

Intellectually, it's very easy to say, "I'm in love with Jesus. Our church is in love with Jesus." Then when you go to a board meeting or business meeting, you never even hear his name. You go to the worship service, and people are more concerned with presentation and the occasion's entertainment value than with their connection to Jesus.

Ask yourself what you love more than you love Jesus. Jesus said, "If you love me, you'll do it. If you love me, you'll follow my commandments. If you love me, you'll feed my sheep." Love is the mechanism that will release the church into the world. We'll follow the one we love. As we love Christ, we discover the church. Falling in love with Jesus changes the expressions and practices of the church.

We once held a Sunday night worship-and-prayer service with no agenda other than to praise God for being God and to thank Jesus for being Jesus. We took a risk and set up an open microphone. About four hundred folks gathered for this event. The simple instructions were to pray and give thanks to Jesus for who he is. We planned to conclude with praise, song, and reflection. But, guess what. We couldn't do it. As soon as people came to the microphone, they began talking about how *they* had done this and *they* had discovered that. I realized we had become so absorbed in what Jesus does for *us* that it's very difficult to simply express our love to him.

I often wonder if we've tried so hard to be profound and sophisticated that we've forgotten how to simply be in love. I find that the congregation I pastor is more lifted up, not when I'm preaching some profound revelation of God, but when I am simply revealing the nature and love of Jesus. I recently preached a sermon about the woman named Mary who opened an expensive jar of perfume and poured its contents on Jesus' feet (John 12:1-7). She got it. She understood it. She was a part of an intimate moment. She was willing to give it up. The fragrance of her sacrifice was more exquisite than the fragrance of the oil.

The beginning of my marriage lacked intimacy because I didn't know how to be like Mary and just open myself up. I was trying to *prove* myself to my wife. I was trying to prove to her that she had made a good decision. I tried to make up for my misbehavior by an outward act. If I'd yelled or in another way lacked grace, I'd buy her something. But the gift didn't seem to touch her. What really touched my wife was when I reached out to hold her hand. Her reaction puzzled me.

One day, I asked, "Why do you like me to hold your hand? It's so simple, but you get so excited about it."

"Because it lets me know that you love me. When you do it without being expected to, it reminds me that you love me." In the same way, the church finds new life as it discovers the surprising ways God loves us.

The church finds new life as it discovers the surprising ways God loves us.

Passion Point

Now, think about it. What do you love more than Jesus? What affair are you carrying on right now? From what other source are you trying to find intimacy, energy, passion, joy, and peace? I'm convinced that at the feet of Jesus we will unlock the mystery of the community of faith. Why do we do almost anything to avoid the feet of Jesus?

When I began my ministry in 1991 at Hillvue, I was forced to go to the inward experience of Jesus Christ, because all the outward trappings of ministry had been shattered. This experience taught me that when our image of what church should be or could be is shattered, Jesus' image of true community can emerge. Love emerges in us. Love discovers us more than we discover it. Because Jesus has found us worthy and loves us, we can love him. We are reshaped by the love of Jesus. The church called Hillvue Heights Church began to grow, living out the message that Jesus loves us and because Jesus loves us, we can be reshaped. Love reshapes us. It reforms us. Sin deforms us, but the love of Jesus transforms us.

Wedding Checklist

1. What does your church really love? You can find out simply by identifying how its dollars are spent. That's where its heart is.

2. How can you begin to up the celebration ante in your church? When people enter into marriage with Jesus, how can you help them enjoy the moment?

3. How can you gauge the authenticity of your congregation's connection to Jesus?

4. How does your church demonstrate the unity of the kingdom of God in your community?

5. Do the practices of your church reflect its passion for Jesus Christ?

Marriage:

Keeping the Embers Burning

So how can the church keep the marital embers burning? Just as people in a physical marriage do, the church must constantly return to the experiences that make for a vibrant, healthy relationship. Five experiences will stoke the marriage flame in any church. They'll help people live out their marriage with Jesus and develop their faith. At Hillvue we call them "the big five that keep you alive." These five experiences are described in Acts 2. They are worship, teaching, prayer, service, and relationship.

These elements are intimately connected. When we worship, we're taught. When we worship, we pray. When we pray, we worship. When we worship, we serve God. Serving God is an act of worship. Building relationships is an act of worship. Worship is an intimate moment with God in which we are reminded that we do love God with all our heart, mind, soul, and body. Because of this, we can love our neighbors as ourselves.

Worship

I define worship as sharing the passion that comes from knowing Jesus Christ as Lord. Worship isn't just presentation. It isn't structure. It isn't just proclamation. It's those moments in our lives when we come to the revealed understanding that Jesus Christ loves us and we express our love to Jesus. It's a romantic moment with God. It's when we surrender ourselves and just love God. Worship is Jesus-centered.

Worship can be *expressed* through a multitude of activities. I'm not so concerned about reviewing expressions of worship as I am with making sure we understand that worship is on a continuum and not just a moment. I worship God in all that I do. There is a rhythm to worship. God is in the house, and because God is in the house, expressions of worship begin to flow. Our connection to God should create energy. Love creates energy. Worship is about honoring God and expressing our love to him. It's about surrendering and understanding that Jesus is Lord, Jesus is the centerpiece, Jesus is life—Jesus is everything. We are declaring in worship, "Lord, I have surrendered to your way." Worship moves us to discover the love of God.

Worship should be celebrative at times. We need to celebrate that we're in love with God. In physical marriages, we celebrate anniversaries and other special occasions that signal our love. I cannot express to you how important it is that we learn to celebrate in the church as well.

One of my church's ways of celebrating our love for God is to take the whole church camping for a weekend. For three days, we celebrate the joy of knowing God. It's a continuous worship experience. We worship in the way we welcome one another. We worship in the way we help one another set up tents. We worship in the way we relate to one another. We worship in the way we connect with people who are not connected with our body of Christ.

We can express our worship of God in many ways, but the structure of worship isn't as important as the attitude of worship. I have participated in high-church, free-church, charismatic, and non-charismatic models. I have seen the passion and power of God expressed in all these models and more. The way we express our worship is a matter of preference. What is more important is worship connection.

Does your preferred style of worship lead and connect people to an understanding of the love, grace, and nature of God? As they worship God, are people experiencing his grace? We evaluate our worship experiences by listening to the people afterward. We ask them what they discovered, what they heard, what they learned. We ask them how they will be different as a result of their experience. Worship should encourage us to live the life of Jesus. Worship should also empower us to stay in our connection with Jesus so that we reveal his grace to the world around us.

Do other people know where your congregation has been after a worship experience at your church? Do they see the results of worshipping God? If I take a vacation in the winter and bask on the white sands of a warm, sunshiny beach, people will know where I have been when I return. In the same way, people will know I've been with God after I've experienced his love. Real worship leaves evidence.

All the time, people ask me, "Is Hillvue Heights Church built on worship?"

I say, "No. It's built on the death and resurrection of Jesus Christ, but we worship fervently because we believe that Jesus forgives and provides new life. It's the message of Christ that causes us to worship God."

Jesus always sought to glorify the Father. It was his understanding, his message, and his purpose to usher in the glory of God and provide a connection to God. Worship allows us to glorify God. The more we surrender, the more we understand. Worship is a visible expression of our inner feelings toward God and may be manifested in celebration, reflection, stillness, listening, speaking, proclaiming, reading God's Word, colors, imagery, pictures, artistry, drama, and dance.

I encourage you to allow worship to take on many different expressions. In this day of multigenerational churches and multi-task people, we need to focus on the attitude of worship and not its systematic expression. Use what connects. I would never tell a church how to worship, just as I wouldn't tell a couple how to romance each other. Worshipping in a congregation is a romantic moment with God. Own how you worship and who you are in Christ. Do not apologize for how you worship.

At Hillvue, we are very celebrative. We are also quiet and reflective. Our worship illustrates that we're on a journey with God. It shows that anything can happen on this journey at any time. It declares the consistency of God by declaring constantly that people are loved by Jesus and that they can be touched by his joy, express his joy, and know the peace of God.

Worship isn't just the service on Sunday, Wednesday night, Saturday night, or whenever you decide to gather. Worship is the experience of surrendering oneself to God in daily life. Let's apply that concept. Do your work relationships illustrate that you worship God? Does your church structure illustrate that you worship God?

Worship should be consistently connected to everyday life. I've been amazed at how many times we might have a powerful worship experience and then see an argument explode in the parking lot over who's going to exit first. In our culture, we view worship as a moment and not a lifestyle. But if I truly worship something, I follow it. I participate in it. I engage in it. It's on my mind. It's in my thoughts. It shapes who I am.

I used to be an avid water-skier. I loved water-skiing. I was dedicated to water-skiing. In fact, every March I would find myself in freezing cold water, putting on a water ski. When you love something, it shapes your actions. It shapes your nature. It shapes your being. Worship causes you to get caught up in God's moment. You become crazy in love with him. Worship becomes that continuum of moments when you realize your connection with God.

Worship should amaze and awe us. We should be in awe of God. We ought to worship with such fervor that we can't wait to get back to the next worship experience. In our church, we've discovered that, when people are released to worship, to connect in worship, and to declare the love of Jesus, they want to come back. When they are given the freedom to communicate, they want to come back. They love being around passionate worship that reveals the mystery of God.

Sometimes, people ask, "What are you all doing? What's going on at the altar? Why do some people raise their hands? Why do some people not raise their hands?"

I answer, "God is in the house. People are awed by God, and they respond. How they express their awe is as individual as their hairstyles and clothing."

Sometimes when my wife just walks by, I see her beauty as if for the first time. I see her love. I am reminded that she's with me, that she's stayed with me, that she loves me. And I am in awe. In the same way, just looking at a Bible can inspire awe. Inside that book is the story of the Jesus who loves me. We see a cross and stand amazed. We hear the word *grace* and say,

Passion Point

What inspires awe in your congregation? What inspires awe in you? Are you awed by the knowledge that Jesus Christ loves you?

"Amazing." Worship celebrates God, shows us the love of God, reminds us of our connection with God, allows us to experience intimacy with God, declares the glory of God, and empowers us to follow the truths of God.

Passion Point

Think about the worship experiences in your church. Do they remind participants of God's abiding love, and does this inspire their awe? Are people empowered as a result of their worship?

Preacher, do you dread Sundays, or are you glad that God has given you a message to share? Singers, are you ready to sing because you know the glory of God will be expressed through your songs? Those of you who hand out the elements of the Lord's Supper, do you realize that you hold the cup and the bread that remind us that we are all a part of the body of Christ?

As leaders, our task during worship experiences is strictly to provide the environment for the experience. I encourage every church leader to get as many people as possible involved in preparing others to encounter God. This creates a real sense of community and builds relationships.

I pray that your church will become a worshipping church. I pray that your church will experience worship in everything it does. Followers of Christ need empowering worship to realize that God is moving and releasing his church. As the Lord is lifted up in worship, he will lift up the church. As the church lifts up the message of Jesus Christ, all people will draw unto him. This has been the power of Hillvue. People ask me all the time, "Why do so many different people of various backgrounds come to your church?"

I have one response. "If Jesus is lifted up, *he* will draw all people unto him."

It's very difficult to generate energy in a marriage without romance, and it's just as difficult to have power in the church without worship. Heartfelt worship brings people to Christ, no matter what. I have participated in worship experiences that have led to connections with Christ before the preaching even began. We at Hillvue try to allow God to do *his* thing, because his thing has gone way past our plans.

We try to allow God to do **his** *thing, because his thing has gone way past our plans.*

Teaching

We've lived through the information age. Sociologists now tell us that we're moving from the information age and that those with the edge are those who know how to *process* the information. With so much information out there, it is those who can *engage* the information who have the advantage.

It's critical that the church *engage* in the teachings of Jesus and not just *espouse* information about him. What is Jesus teaching us? He reminds us again and again, "Love one another as I have loved you." This is the function of the church.

We need to follow his teachings. Do you know how I know the Bible is true? It's not through some intellectual or didactical argument. It's because I've found that *any* time I have not practiced the truths Jesus declares, the results have been exactly as he said they'd be. We need

Passion Point

I encourage you to evaluate your worship experiences. Do the people in your congregation engage with Jesus in such a way that they are empowered to live as Jesus calls them to live? Do the worship experiences in your church lead the people to reflect the love of Jesus to others?

to be careful in the church. We need to hear Jesus' warnings, especially when he asks, "What good is it for a man to gain the whole world, yet forfeit his soul?" (Mark 8:36). The teachings of Christ engage our souls and cause us to move in the direction of God. Teaching allows us to develop the life in Christ that we've been given. What happens after we meet Jesus? We live. We worship. We abide in the teachings of Jesus. We don't just *espouse* them. We *dwell* in them.

We abide in the teachings of Jesus. We don't just espouse *them. We* dwell *in them.*

Passion Point

Think about the teachings of your church. What do you teach people to do? Do you teach them to be loving? Do you teach them to be inclusive? Do you teach them to be empowering? Or do you just tell stories?

Teaching causes the church to be fruitful. Teaching allows us to become that good soil, so that, when the truth of God is planted in us, we can multiply thirty, sixty, even one hundred times. The teachings of Jesus reveal the life that is within us. I see teaching as a combination of information, experience, and activity, all rolled into one. We must have the information so we can engage in the experience, which should lead us to the activity.

The Lord tells us to "Go ye, therefore" and teach and preach. I have the information. Now, I begin to share my faith. My faith leads me to the experience, which leads me to the activity of evangelism.

The Word tells me to worship only the Lord my God. I discover that when I think about Jesus, focus on Jesus, worship Jesus, and praise Jesus, I surrender and stay in the ways of Jesus. When I am distracted, my thoughts are consumed by everything but Jesus, and I'm more worried about what's going on in the church than about my relationship with Jesus. I become restless and unfocused. Then God reminds me to listen to him: "Love the Lord your God" and worship only him.

Like Jesus, we need to teach through experiences. Let people share the results of following God's truth in their lives. We need to state, declare, sing, and teach God's truth in as many ways as possible.

Early in our marriage, one of our fights was over housecleaning. I cleaned the car and I cleaned the boat, but I wouldn't clean the house. My wife would say, "Would you please straighten up? I have to work late tonight."

"Sure, honey. I will. I know this is important to you." I must have said that a thousand times.

But when I actually did what I had promised to do, the results were completely different from the results of merely talking about it. The same is true of the teachings of God. It isn't enough to just hear the Word of God. We must follow it. We must live it out. We must put it into effect in our lives. It works.

One teaching that we need to emphasize in our churches is that we must surrender those things that kill us. Jesus teaches us to be done with hatred. We need to be done with it. We need to let it go. Jesus teaches us not to be jealous, bitter, or angry. He tells us not to let the sun go down on our anger. He tells us to be loving, joyful, peaceful, patient, kind, and self-controlled. Follow the teachings of Christ. It will give you and your church new life.

Pick up the Word of God. Read it. You'd be amazed at how many people in your church have never read the Bible. It may be amazing how little they know about the life of Jesus. Preach the Bible. Teach the Bible. Talk about the Bible. Tell people the stories of Jesus. They shape us. They mold us. They lead us into a full and abundant life. Constantly teach the Word of God through Bible studies, connection groups, and relationship-building groups. In everything you do, expose people to the Word of God.

One year, I was frustrated that so many in the church didn't know the gospel, who Jesus is, or what he did. I decided to preach the Gospel of Mark, word for word, story for story, and episode for episode. I told the congregation we were going on a journey with the Gospel of Mark. We started in February and ended about a year and a half later. You may wonder, "Did the people get fed? Were they nourished? Was that a complete diet of faith development for them?" Over four hundred people decided to follow Jesus during that time. We tell people to follow Christ's example, but that's impossible if they don't know anything about his life.

We tell people to follow Christ's example, but that's impossible if they don't know anything about his life.

Passion Point

What has Jesus taught us? Love one another. What else has he taught us? Get rid of those things that will kill us, focusing instead on the things that bring us life. Loving people is teaching them about things that will bring them life, not death.

We need to get back to teaching the *Bible*. Sometimes it seems we teach everything but the Bible. I don't need examples from the newspaper on Sunday morning. I need to know what Jesus is calling me to do. What are his teachings? What are his principles? What are his truths?

Let's look at three prominent truths in Jesus' teaching. First of all, he says we are to *go*. The church has got to go. He didn't tell us to sit; he told us to go into the world. Be moving constantly and connecting people to Jesus. If you've got it, you want to give it away. When Jesus is moving in your life, you want to share it. It's natural. When you've got a good marriage, you talk about your marriage. When you have a new grandchild, you talk about that child. You *follow* what you've become convinced of, and you espouse what you believe. Do you believe we're to go? Then get going.

Jesus has also told us to *love one another*. People are important to God, so people must be important to the church. We pastors are sometimes totally led astray because we forget that the church's function is to connect people with Jesus. The way we illustrate connection is by our lifestyle. We should be constantly connecting people to Jesus and to the deeper truths of Jesus, teaching them to love God with all they have, to surrender those things that kill them, to stay faithful to God, and to teach the things Jesus has taught us.

These are things that will definitely kill us: hatred, discord, envy, strife, drunkenness, addictions, and sexual immorality. Just get rid of those things! They're killing you! We need to teach the church to stay out of things that kill them, and get into things that bring them life. These are revealed in the teachings of Jesus.

The third thing that Jesus teaches us is that *he's always there*. He's among us. He's coaching us. We need to allow his Spirit to bring us wisdom. His Spirit really works. John 1:14 tells us that "the Word became flesh and made his dwelling among us."

Jesus is among us, and his Holy Spirit leads us to the truth. He reveals the whole story, not selective parts of the Scripture. Spirit-driven teaching allows us to teach with God's authority and thus leads to changed behavior and new life.

I've found that marriage is a much more enjoyable experience when we live it out instead of just talking it out. If my wife told me she loved me but never spent time with me, I'd have trouble believing that she really loved me. When we practice the teachings of Jesus, we deepen our understanding of our relational connection to him.

Prayer

Prayer is another central experience of the church. Prayer allows us to hear God. Pastor, are you praying, or are you reporting to God?

I find that I listen better in a crisis than I do when I'm feeling all right. I've also discovered that if I listened to God more when I was feeling all right, I would experience fewer crises. What is God saying to the church? He is telling us to listen. "He who has ears, let him hear" what God is saying to the church.

Now, I'm not going to tell you what God's saying to you; I don't know. But whatever he tells you will contain this closing: From Jesus, who loves you.

Jesus has instructed me to do things that I thought would not work, but they worked. The church I pastor has been navigated by prayer and listening to God. This means that I have had to give up *my* way to engage in *God's* way.

Relationships get better when we finally learn to listen. Mary knew this secret. She listened to Jesus. She sat there at his feet, simply listening.

What's God saying to you right now? What's he saying to you as you think about worship and the teachings of God? What's he saying to you when you think about prayer? I encourage you to make prayer an experience in which you hear from God. Whatever Jesus tells you to do, go do it. The greatest model for prayer is hearing God, then lifting up that message to God. In prayer, we learn to praise God. In prayer, we learn the character and nature of God. In prayer, we hear God's instructions.

As you pray, begin to praise God for what's going on. Thank God that you're a pastor. Thank God for allowing you to be a church leader. Thank God for the congregation he's given you, even if it's full of knuckleheads. Thank God that you get to preach his Word with passion every Sunday, Wednesday night, Thursday night, Saturday night, or whenever. You get to declare the glory of God. Thank God that you're forgiven! Thank God that you can share in his glory! Thank God that you've been called to an inheritance greater than you can even imagine!

Then listen to God's instructions. Prayer is power. It's hearing the voice of God. It renews our minds, instructs the church, and gives us new life. The voice of God calms the storm. A praying pastor will be a pastor who celebrates full and abundant life with his congregation. A pastor who lacks the willingness to listen to God will soon be a pastor who is burned out, dried up, or just mechanically producing religious activity.

When I listen to God, I am brought to the deepest understanding that God's power is greater than any other power I can experience. *God is in the house.* God is in your life. Pray constantly, and do what God says, even when you don't understand it.

Prayer causes us to move in directions we wouldn't otherwise consider. While he was at the wedding celebration in Cana, Jesus asked the servants to fill the water jars so the guests might have wine. That's an illogical way to get wine, but the servants listened to what Jesus said rather than what their logic told them. Thus, they were able to get beyond their logic and into Jesus' reality.

Prayer allows us to connect with the reality of the Spirit. That's why Jesus tells us to pray for our enemies. It's risky, because someone who was once an enemy might just become a friend. An even greater risk is that those who used to be enemies might just become brothers and sisters. Pray for one another, and pray for your enemies.

On April 16, 1998, we had a horrendous hailstorm in Bowling Green. The hailstorm knocked the windows out of our church and bent the roof. People were stunned.

In the midst of that chaos, a man stormed into my office in a rage. He was distraught because his son's car, which had been in the church parking lot, had been destroyed along with his drums, which were in the back of the car. I told him that I didn't create the storm and didn't cause his son to drive to church and leave his car parked there.

As he cursed and yelled, he got right in my face. Two other pastors stood beside me, and I felt a swelling anger reminiscent of everything I used to be. I used to love to play football, and I didn't mind hitting a fellow. I felt that rage and anger, but in that moment I remembered a teaching and worship experience we had just had on Sunday about loving our enemies. I thought, "Lord, please, if he hits me, don't let it hurt too bad. If he hits me, Lord, I want to act the way you would and not the way I would." As my blood pressure rose, I thought, "Dear Lord, please show him your love."

By a miracle from God, I was able to be still and not react in anger. I didn't know how violent the man could get. I thought that in order to subdue him, I would have to remove my pastor's hat. I didn't have to do that. I looked him straight in the eyes and said, "Sir, all I know in a moment like this is Jesus." Stunned, he got back into his car and drove off. Two days later, I received a letter in which he apologized for his actions. A week later, he came by the office and talked to me. A couple of weeks later, he trusted Jesus Christ as his Lord and Savior. How true are the teachings of Jesus?

I could never have reacted as I did if a wave of prayer hadn't been moving in my life. My human nature does not allow me to accept such behavior. My nature in Christ, empowered by prayer, has the ability to turn the other cheek and declare to the world that Jesus Christ is everything. Pray about everything, every move you make, every decision you face, and every person you encounter. Let us learn to pray *for* one another. Don't just tritely say, "Well, I'm praying for you, brother. May God bless you." Let's lift one another up. We need to pray for the sick. We need to pray for the disconnected. We need to pray for the connected. We need to pray for churches. We need to pray for churches that are building the kingdom of God. When we pray for one another, we come together. Prayer deepens our awareness of the impact of Christ on the community.

We need to pray with our spouses because prayer deepens intimacy. It allows the Spirit of God to speak softly and gently to our souls. The toughest thing I do is pray with my wife. When I pray with her, I know my true self is going to be revealed. But the great news about prayer is that Jesus is revealed as well.

Pray without ceasing. Pray all kinds of prayers. Pray for those who preach, teach, and admonish. Pray for those who participate in the church. Pray for those who are disconnected from the church. Pray for those who have yet to believe in Jesus. I believe you have gotten the point. *Always be praying.*

Service

We need to rediscover servanthood in the life of the church. Christians do not exist to be served. Early in our marriage, when I thought my wife should do everything for me, I hadn't discovered marriage. By the same token, Christians who demand that the church serve them are missing the point.

Christ came to serve, and the bride of Christ is also a servant. "Humble yourselves before the Lord" (James 4:10). "Blessed are the meek, for they will inherit the earth" (Matthew 5:5). "God opposes the proud and gives grace to the humble" (1 Peter 5:5). Humility doesn't require that we disregard the talents and gifts we've been given. It doesn't mean that we can't do a wonderful job. It doesn't mean that we can't appear successful. It means that, in all we do, we are to give the glory to God.

As the church, we must show God's kindness to everybody. Kindness changes people. Kindness brings people to an understanding of Jesus. Jesus is kind. Jesus is always welcoming, serving, and preparing for people. When all those people were hungry, it was kind of Jesus to bless the loaves and fish and feed everyone. Jesus is the servant who provides for our needs, and he wants us to be servants also. If you'll follow him, you will serve him.

Is your church a serving church? Is it a church with a selfless attitude that proclaims, "We're here to experience God. We want you to experience God. We want you to know it's all about God"? We must be careful to remember that service is all about God. Some churches worship the act of service and not the ultimate Servant. The reason we're serving isn't that we're overly moral, super-blessed, good people. It's because Christ has shown us kindness, and we reflect that kindness to the world. Serve God with all your heart. It's through acts of servanthood that people begin to understand Jesus.

At Hillvue, we love being servants to the community. We have fun doing it. We're that church that will do it when nobody else will—whether it's landscaping a sign in front of the city or replacing roof shingles on a poor person's home. When you learn to serve others, those who don't know Jesus will take notice.

Encourage the people in your church to serve. Don't just serve the church; serve people. Jesus served people—and not just the people in the synagogue. He served the people of the world. Church, if there's something we lack in a big way, it's busting the gospel message forth in the world through the power of servanthood.

Why is it that Christians can be some of the most obnoxious and selfish human beings around? It should be the opposite. People ought to say, "I just met some folks who follow Jesus. They are kind. They are gentle. They are loving. They are accepting. They are firm in their beliefs, but loving to my spirit." That's the attitude of servanthood.

Jesus tells us in Matthew 25 that when the Son of Man comes in all his glory, he will know those who truly "got it." It won't be their servanthood that brought them to God but their relationship with God that brought them into servanthood. When the Son of Man comes in all his glory, he's going to put those people on his right and say, "You did it. You ushered in the kingdom. The reason you're a part of the kingdom of God is you were *always* a part of the kingdom of God. You engaged in the actions of the kingdom of God."

When I first came to Hillvue, the church had no money. People would come by and say, "Can you give me something to eat?"

I would say, "We've got five dollars. We can give you gas to get you to a church that can give you something to eat. How's that?" We'd call ahead to another church and say, "Hey, maybe someday we'll have some money, but right now, we don't have any money. We've got five dollars to put some gas in someone's car to get him to you. Can you help him?" We've always tried to help everybody in some way, which may sometimes seem naive. But I've found that it's better to help people than to wonder if you're being taken advantage of.

Look at what Jesus said. "When I was hungry, you gave me something to eat. When I was a stranger, you invited me in." One of the greatest acts of servanthood is invitation. Think about your church. Is it an inviting place? Does it welcome people, saying, "Come here. We want you to know that Jesus loves you, and we want you to know that we love you. We're really glad you're here"? This is one of the main reasons that people have come to our church.

I ask people all the time, "Why do you come to Hillvue?"

They answer, "I'm welcomed here. I feel accepted here. You know, I can come as I am. When I came here, I was broken-down and busted up. When I came here, I was rich and arrogant. You welcomed me as I was. Your church just said, 'Come.' "

114 *Marriage:* Keeping the Embers Burning

Servanthood isn't an activity that *makes* us righteous; servanthood is the activity in which righteous people engage. Let everybody do something to help someone in the life of your church. Everyone can be a part of inviting someone. Even in our worship service, we say, "Everybody here is going to have to be a greeter for a moment. We want you to welcome the people next to you. We want you to welcome them into the presence of God. We want you to let them know this morning that they're welcome to experience Jesus, no matter where they've been or who they are. They're welcome here. Turn to the person next to you and just say, 'Welcome. We're glad you're here.'"

Jesus is glad we're here. Jesus is glad we decided to be a part of his body. He has invited all people in.

Here's an overwhelming thought: Jesus is glad we're here. Jesus is glad we decided to be a part of his body. He has invited all people in. Welcome people. Give clothes to people. Visit the sick and those in prison. Make sure you take care of the least of these. Also remember that sometimes the least of these drive Jaguars. Sometimes, the least of these aren't just those who are without money; they are those without the Spirit. Never forget that you can profit the whole world and lose your soul. Never forget, church, that we're a soul-seeking community. We want people to know that their souls can be connected to Jesus Christ and that they never have to be the same.

The greatest way to be a servant is to live it out. Live it out. Then, tell people, "I just want you to know the love of Jesus. I can't make you love Jesus. I can't make you accept this message, but I want you to know the love of Jesus." There are some people in our church who won't quit. They keep loving people who continue to reject them. In fact, one guy told me, "These people made me so mad because for five years they loved me. They kept loving me and loving me no matter what I did. Then came the day I realized that this must be real. My actions should have run them off by then. They must have something greater in them than themselves."

Servanthood begins to illustrate that the grace of God isn't just a theological and philosophical concept. The grace of God is activated as we reach out to others, serve others, and lift others up. We activate grace when we honor God. Serve others, for by this, people will know that you love God. Jesus said, "By your love, they will know that you are my disciples" (John 13:35, paraphrased).

In the midst of doing church, filling out reports, examining attendance records, checking budgets, doing funerals, and arranging weddings, it's too easy to get trapped and lose sight of the people. Leaders who are servants lead churches to serve. It's vital that we leaders involve ourselves in servanthood.

Relationship

Finally, the church is called to connect people through relationship. It's a three-way relationship: We are connected to God through Jesus Christ. We're connected to one another in Jesus Christ. Then, because we are married to Jesus, we're to connect to the world. We're not just observing marriage. We're not just thinking about being married. We are married. We are *in* a marriage, and that means we are *in* a relationship.

Our relationship with Jesus Christ shapes us into loving, joyful, and peaceful people. It causes us to be concerned for others. It makes us want to worship God. It encourages us to go beyond human reason and human logic and to do what God tells us to do. It causes us to recognize the reality of other people's needs. This is our story. It's the story of grace.

To the world, we in the church are to demonstrate the reality of grace. Jesus is the invisible made visible. We in the church are the invisible message of grace made visible. We are to be with one another. We are to devote ourselves to teaching. We're to devote ourselves to the things we have in common, even to the point that we would sell our possessions for the greater good of the community. We are to break bread and to praise God, learning to enjoy the favor of all the people. When we learn to build our relationship with Christ, engaging in it, living in it, staying with it, and being empowered by it, we will be others-focused. The community of Christ is a wonderful place to live! Henri Nouwen talks about what we reveal to others as we drink from the cup: "It is not enough to claim our sorrow and joy in silence. We also must claim them in a trusted circle of friends. To do so we need to speak about what is in our cup."[1]

I encourage you to invite *all* people to your church. Hillvue is a place for all people. It's a place for people who have a lot of money and for those who don't. It's a place for people of different skin colors. It's a place for people of different sociological backgrounds. I've discovered in the past twelve years that my affinity group will teach me less about Jesus than the groups with whom I'm unfamiliar.

I've been amazed at the creativity of people I never expected to see in church. I have been so amazed to hear the profound theology of mechanics

Passion Point

Think about your church. Think about the people you share church with. Think about those relationships. Aren't they glorious? Aren't they marvelous? Aren't they wonderful? Don't they connect you with the love of God? Don't they begin to illustrate the stability of grace? Aren't you glad to know that you can accept people and invite them to experience this grace?

and steel workers as well as professionals and theologians. I've been so amazed to find the nature of God in the simple places as well as the complex places. That's the beautiful mosaic of authentic Christian community.

To pull all five experiences together we must engage in three connections. One, we need to talk to one another. Communicate who you are and be willing to reveal your thoughts and your personal history. Two, we need to listen. We need to listen to people's stories. We need to learn where they're from, what makes them tick, why they think as they do, and what has shaped their lives. Three, we need to tell the story of Jesus. He pulls us all together. Relationships that are based in Christ last forever.

I pray that we as the church will reflect the everlasting God by living out our relationship with Jesus Christ with fervent worship, engaging teachings, illustrative servanthood, listening and prayerful hearts, and relationships with others that cause them to know that we are all a part of Jesus' story.

Are you married? Are you practicing? Are you on the journey? Is the journey unfolding in your church? Just remember that all moments—*all* moments—show us God. The bitter moments, joyful moments, bored moments, and exciting moments. They're all a part of being married to Christ. We must follow Jesus. When we do, we'll have a full and abundant life.

Wedding Checklist

1. Do you have programming in place to help people sustain their marriage to Jesus?

2. List all the ways that your church invites people to marry Jesus. Is your net wide enough?

3. What would happen if your church returned to the five basic experiences of the church?

4. Carefully consider what it means to truly worship God. Are you satisfied that genuine worship is reflected in your life and that of your church?

5. When you pray, do you do all the talking? How much listening do you really do?

Pleasure:

Leading the Bride's Heart

Jesus says, "I come that you might have full and abundant life" (John 10:10, paraphrased). Is your church abundant? Is it full of worship? Is it full of Jesus' teachings? Is it full of an attitude of service? Is it full of healthy relationships? Does it illustrate a life of communion and prayer? Following Jesus will lead to a full and abundant life, both individually and corporately.

Jesus leads us to a place of freedom, not a place of burden. I hear people refer to marriage as "the ol' ball and chain." They think that once they get married, their freedom will end. Just the opposite is true. Marriage to Jesus and to a spouse is intended to be full, abundant, and filled with pleasure. Galatians 5 tells us that when we live in the Spirit, we finally find freedom. And in that freedom, we find pleasure.

Let's explore the pleasures of leading the bride in the twenty-first century. Far from being the worst era of ministry, I believe it can be the very best time to be in church leadership.

The Pleasure of an Exciting Present and Future

Church leaders need to view the church as a current event and stop longing for the past days of the church. I'm tired of hearing about "the good old days." I'm tired of hearing about the 1950s, huge church-attendance numbers, and the surge of evangelism. I truly believe that the best days of the church are yet to come as she realizes all that can come from her connection to Christ.

The best days of the church are yet to come as she realizes all that can come from her connection to Christ.

What do you need to do to allow the full and abundant life of Jesus Christ to be reflected in your church? It doesn't matter what worship styles you use; what matters is that the worship you give be full of life. Every time you teach the Bible, that teaching ought to lead people to a better life. Leading passionate people isn't about performance; it's about lives. Is it time to change your perspective?

The Pleasure of Mission

Do you know what kills pleasure in ministry? Mechanics. Do you know what enthralls us in ministry? Mission. It's easy to get trapped in the mechanics of ministry and miss the mission of God. It's easy to get hung up on execution and presentation.

At Hillvue Heights Church, we've learned that presentation isn't as important as participation. We want to know that we're participating in the worship of God. We want to be sure we're participating in prayer with God. God wants to be *in* us. And he wants to come *out* of us so others might know that they, too, are loved and can be radically changed by God.

Ours is a covenant of freedom. For too long, I found the church to be a place of burden, confinement, and boredom. The opposite is true when we abide in the Lord Jesus Christ. We find freedom in our connection with Jesus. His commandments are not burdensome.

Allow God's covenant to set you free. He tells us, "It is for freedom that Christ has set us free. Stand firm, then, and do not let yourselves be burdened again by a yoke of slavery" (Galatians 5:1). Isn't it great that God has called the church into an intimate covenant, not a burdensome routine, with himself?

Passion Point

How are you living with Christ? Is your life alluring to those who are not connected to Jesus? Would someone look at you and say, "You know, I want to have a life like yours because I see the full and abundant life of Jesus Christ pouring out of you"?

Isn't it great that God has called the church into an intimate covenant, not a burdensome routine, with himself?

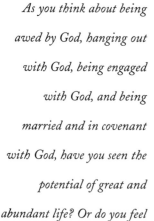
This is the truth that sets us free: God loves human beings. He said so when he sent his Son to die on a cross and to rise from the grave. In our church, we constantly ask, "Do you get it?" *Do* you get it? If so, it's time to live it. We truly don't understand God until we're willing to live inside his covenant relationship.

You'll never dance by reading a book on dancing. You'll never preach by studying preaching techniques. You'll never understand the intimacy of relationship until you risk engaging in one. Will you be hurt? Yes, you will. Will you be healed? Yes, you will. Is being intimate with God worth the risk? Yes. Once we give it up, get it on, and live it large, the pain of human disappointment can in no way compare to the richness of the great possibilities God offers.

Once we give it up, get it on, and live it large, the pain of human disappointment can in no way compare to the richness of the great possibilities God offers.

The Pleasure of Joy in the Ministry

God wants to refresh the leaders of his church. It's time for us to put joy back into the ministry. It's time for us to love more than we work. It's time for us to be in relationship with God instead of running God's business.

Jesus always had time for people. Do you? Jesus always had time for intimate moments. Do you? Jesus had time to stop and let the children play on his lap. What about you? Do you have time to know the names of the children who walk and run in your church's hallways? Or does the next book you're going to write, the next sermon you're going to preach, or the next praise and worship set occupy far more of your mind than the people you serve?

This generation doesn't want to hear our words; it wants to see our faith in our lives. "Does it work? Is it real? Is it possible? Can I feel it? Can I touch it? Can I be a part of it?" The answer to each of these questions is a resounding "Yes!" God loves us, and he sent his Son into the world, not to condemn us, but to save, rescue, and enter into a covenant with us (John 3:16-17, paraphrased). This astounding realization makes us new.

This generation doesn't want to hear our words; it wants to see our faith in our lives. "Does it work? Is it real? Is it possible? Can I feel it? Can I touch it? Can I be a part of it?"

Each day with God is new, just as each day in a marriage is new. If you choose to be single, which God honors, each day in your friendships and other relationships is new. The church is in a constant state of change because it's in relationship.

People at Hillvue often ask me, "What's next?"

I say, "I'm not sure what's next, but I know what will be happening. God will be loving people."

I have become totally convinced that if we will love people, practice our faith, love God's church, and participate in the church, we'll understand God's heart.

It is for freedom that he has set us free. Are you free? Can you go home and love your spouse? As you preach, do you feel God's possibility in your heart and does what you feel speak through your lips? Do you participate daily in a community that sets you free?

Maybe you need to be reminded occasionally that God put you in this position and that your part in the body of Christ is to lead others into an intimate relationship with Jesus Christ. It's tough to teach and preach about intimacy if you don't live intimately with Jesus.

As a pastor, I can be full of words, but I'm amazed when *the Word* fills me. When I'm full of religious words, empty experiences await me. When *the Word* fills me, my words are usually shorter, more concise, definitely a lot simpler, and always more freeing.

The Pleasure of Diversity

Passion Point

Can you hear God? Can you hear him telling you, "You're a part of my church"?

In the early days of my ministry, I talked about Jesus, loved Jesus, and was unashamedly convinced of Jesus. Then I went to an institution to be trained in the ministry. During this training, I lost my ability to minister, because the institution didn't understand the method God was going to use to express his truths through me. Institutions prepare us for certain aspects of ministry, and they certainly have value. I'm just not a hair-parted-on-the-side, suit-and-tie-wearing preacher. I'm a preacher who just wants people to know Jesus is *it*.

I don't care how you bring people to Jesus, and I don't think Jesus does, either. However you express Jesus, what's important is that people know Jesus. Do they sense his presence, and do they stand in awe of it?

Be reminded that you're a part of God's awe-inspiring work. Be refreshed again by the amazing grace of God. Fall in love all over again.

In the beginning of my ministry, people told me I would lose my excitement. I listened to them, and it happened. I lost my desire and became a mechanical, preaching, Bible-studying machine able to produce curriculum, talks, and sermons like a factory. I preached, but I didn't see much of God's activity. I spoke, but nobody heard. Have you been there? Are you there now?

In 1987, I fell in love with God again. I said, "Jesus, you're it. You're it, no matter what. You're it, no matter what we say. You're still everything." When Jesus became everything, awe surged back into my life.

The Pleasure of Hanging Out

Church leaders need to hang out again—hang out in the world, that is. We need to listen to people who aren't in church. We need to show them that Jesus has healed us and encourage them to believe he will heal them, too. When people walk into your church on a Sunday morning, do they find a place of life, hope, and possibility? As a few people with train-wrecked lives begin to walk full and abundant lives, you won't have to put out any marketing bulletins for your church. People will come.

As a few people with train-wrecked lives begin to walk full and abundant lives, you won't have to put out any marketing bulletins for your church.

If there's life inside your church, people will come to taste it, get it, and live in it. You'll have a few critics, but it's a lot easier to take words of criticism when you're living a full and abundant life than when you're in a mundane, routine, methodical ministry. Jesus speaks words of life. We need to be hanging out in the world, simply speaking the words of life.

God calls us to have a great faith. He calls us, not to be great people, but to be connected to him. When it's all said and done, wouldn't it be better to be remembered as one who loved Jesus? If you love Jesus, you'll understand the greater things of life. The trappings of the twentieth century have lured many church leaders away from simply loving Jesus, being married to Jesus, and realizing that other people are also part of the bride.

Many in the church have been trapped by a kind of celebrity Christianity. In the '80s, many church leaders thought bigger was better: "If the congregation is large, then it must be alive." Not necessarily. The large congregation might just be a large group of people doing large things for themselves.

Want to know what makes a powerful church? When people walk in and sense an intimacy with God and the freedom that comes from it, the church is powerful. Apparently Jesus wasn't too impressed with crowds. He said that where two or more are gathered, "...there am I" (Matthew 18:20). It's his presence that makes the difference, not ours.

The mere trappings of religion will not bring the movement of God. Displaying crosses, reading Bibles, and saying prayers to save our own souls will not connect us to the movement of God. It's when we realize that Jesus Christ wants to be in us and with us and to work through us that awe explodes in us. It's about full life. Joy and sorrow. Laughter and mourning. Dancing and stillness. Victory and defeat. God is in all of them. That's the great hope.

The power of God is revealed in the church. If the church were make-believe and only existed by human strategy and human power, if it were only connected to human tradition and human thought, it would have been destroyed by now. The church has looked almost defeated at times, but no one has been able to get rid of it. You can shove it out of a country, but it will go underground and become stronger. You can make it large, small, ecstatic, or dull. It is still the church, and that church reigns.

That church is not empowered by institutional structures, denominational approval, systematic preachers, or theological understandings. That church is not made great because of the deeds it has done for the world. All these are important, but they are simply illustrations of a deeper truth.

Remember that church in Ephesus. It did great things. It was structured in great ways. It did deeds for God. But then the angel said, "This I have against you. You have lost your first love. Return to it. Remember the height from which you have fallen" (Revelation 2:4-5, paraphrased). In the twelve years I've pastored Hillvue Heights Church, we've been distracted more than once because we lost our first love.

Let me warn you gently. Anytime you begin to love what you do more than what God can do, you will lose the sense of a full and abundant life. The possibilities of the world are in Jesus Christ, not in us. The Jesus that's in us can do all things. We live with a victorious Jesus. When we live *in* that Jesus and when we're in love with that Jesus, we'll illustrate the characteristics of Jesus.

It all boils down to love. Marriage is always about love. Whether my wife and I agree or disagree, whether I've been a wonderful husband, lifting her up as a radiant bride, or just a mule-head the entire day, she still loves me. We're still in a wonderful marriage. Isn't it great to know as church leaders that God loves us even when we get it wrong? His love is what shapes us, what forms us, and what allows us to say, "This is the day the Lord has made. I'm going to rejoice and be glad in it."

Church, it's time for us to be in love with Jesus in such a dramatic way that the world realizes Jesus' love for us. Imagine the day when those who live in America can look at the church, hear the words of the Bible, and see those words reflected in the people who love Jesus. Until we love Jesus, we won't understand the Bible. Until we learn to love each other, we'll never fully understand what it means to love Jesus. Jesus loves people, all of them—rich, poor, black, red, yellow, white, and every combination you can imagine.

I am often asked, "Does your church have a targeted focus?"

I say, "Yes. If you're a human being and have a pulse, we want you to be connected to Jesus." That's been our attitude since Day One. We're not a yuppie church. We're not a Generation X church. We're not a twenty-something church. We're a church that believes that all people can be loved by Jesus. The simplicity of that statement leads us to the complexity of ministry in a diverse church.

Our target: If you're a human being and have a pulse, we want you to be connected to Jesus.

Jesus loves us. It's in that loving relationship that ministry comes forth and that pastors, directors, leaders, denominational leaders, and other participants in the church begin to discover a full and abundant life. We *discover* it through the love of Jesus and through the possibility of Jesus.

What are you discovering? What have you been challenged to do? Think about the disciplines in your life. What do you truly give to God?

What's God saying to you? Do you listen to God? Is there freedom in your ministry? Is there freedom in your church? When new people walk in, do they understand that they can be connected to something greater than themselves?

Maybe instead of trying to meet human needs, we should overcome them with the grace of God. I'm not against meeting human needs, but what humans ultimately need is Jesus. Somebody needs to tell us that again. We need to meet Jesus. Sometimes people meet him through a bowl of soup. Sometimes people meet him as they're being clothed. Sometimes people meet him as they're given five dollars to put gas in a car. People meet Jesus. We meet him in everything we do.

The Pleasure of Love

Life is not about perfection; it's about love. Marriage is about love. Raising children is about love. Families navigate life learning to love. We need to get rid of the word *perfect* in the church and replace it with *love*. Maybe we even need to eliminate the word *successful* in the church. People ask me, "What's a successful ministry?"

I say, "This is it." After twelve years of struggling with the whole concept of success, this could be it. Do the people in your congregation love Jesus as a result of hanging around your church?

We need to get rid of the word **perfect** *in the church and replace it with* **love.** *Maybe we even need to eliminate the word* **successful** *in the church.*

We're never going to figure it all out. I laugh when people tell me their intricate plans for a successful marriage or a successful church. There's no A-B-C order to a full and abundant life; that's a myth. More than once, I've witnessed the despair and agony of parents who attended church regularly, took their kids to Sunday school, made sure their kids were in a youth group, had personal and private devotions with them, and made sure they got all the religious information—only to watch them rebel as teenagers. Why? Because information will not change us until it becomes a part of us. Knowing *about* Jesus is nothing like *knowing* Jesus. Knowing *about* marriage is nothing like being *in* marriage. Knowing *about* the mission of God is nothing like being *in* the mission. It's when God's truth enters us that full and abundant life begins to explode in us.

What's in you? Is it the kingdom of God? Is it the possibility of God? Is it the power of God? Is it Jesus himself who is the head of your church? Doesn't he promise that he'll wash us with holy water, cleanse us, and make us radiant? These words sound like words of life, not words of systematic religion. They're words of celebration, dance, living, and joy. Let the word out. God loves you. He didn't call you to a performance; he called you into a love relationship.

The Pleasure of Intimacy

Where's the mission? The mission is in the marriage, the connection, and the relationship. It's not until you relate that you'll go. Jesus spent a lot of time with his disciples before he ever gave them the Great Commission. The same rhythm should be present in our congregations. It's by spending time with Jesus, understanding his Word, dwelling with him in prayer, being at his feet, breaking open the expensive perfume, and understanding that God is madly in love with us that we'll join in his mission. When we join his mission, we can clothe the naked, visit those in prison, welcome the stranger, and touch the world. We'll become the radiant bride.

I am convinced that intimacy with Christ is the key to moving the church effectively through the twenty-first century. Reason, logic, and study are still important, but they must begin with intimacy with God. We must leave the things that rob our lives—things like anger, bitterness, rage, jealousy, disappointments, and betrayals. We must hold hands with Jesus and listen to him carefully so that he can take away the things that confine us and release in us the things that free us.

I am convinced that intimacy with Christ is the key to moving the church effectively through the twenty-first century.

The mission is in the marriage. It's in the connection with God. Think about it. Feel it. What truly matters is that others fall in love with Jesus and become a part of God's connection, the bride. When they fall in love with Jesus, they'll realize that Jesus is in love with them. When you're in love, you follow.

When I was first married, I never made the bed. I barely cleaned the house. I didn't take care of things. I was rebellious. I was pigheaded. I wasn't gentle, kind, or loving. Elizabeth and I had an upheaval that drove us so far apart that we thought we were no longer connected. Then, at the point of losing my marriage, I realized I was in love. When I realized the depth of my love for my wife, marriage became natural and unforced. Remember the business adage from the '80s, "Fake it 'til you make it"? Have it for real, and you don't have to fake it. There's nothing fake about God.

Once you realize that God literally loves the hell out of you, you'll embrace him and love him. He loves the hellish places out of our lives. He loves the hellish attitudes out of our ministries. He enfolds us in a mission. That's how deep the love of Jesus goes. But don't think that a full and abundant life won't include a little hell.

I know that scares most of us in the church. We're trying to create utopia instead of life. Some churches are so sweet that I want to throw up. The reality of love isn't sweetness; it's that, in the difficult times, *God's still there.* In the peaceful times, *God's still there.* In times of upheaval, *God's still there.* In the midst of the storms, *God's still there.* Even when I feel as if I'm drowning, *God is still there.* Our intimate moments with Jesus will drive us to connect others to Jesus.

Are you in a methodical relationship with Jesus? Are you a functioning leader who spouts quotes, methods, systems, and the latest book you've read? Or are you an intimate lover of Jesus who has a fresh word for others because the Holy Spirit whispered it in your ear? Do you have a fresh word that reminds you that God is pursuing humans and God loves them no matter where they've been? Hope, joy, and peace are realities, not some foreign concept. As you lead, do your constituents know that with Christ all things are possible?

We'll not change the world until we become lovers of Jesus. Jesus has called me to be a lover of his life, a lover of his mission, a lover of his intimacy. There are times that I want to fight for the truth, but the truth doesn't need to be fought for; the truth is in me. The truth isn't a concept; it's a person, a God who became man.

In my ministry, I want life. I want it full. I want it abundant. I want all the gusto. I want everything I can have before I check out. Jesus says, "I am the life. I am the resurrection." He doesn't say, "I was resurrected." He says, "*I am* the resurrection." He is the place of everything.

I hope Jesus is your place of everything. When he is, life emerges—full, abundant, victorious, triumphant, radiant, and intimate life. I don't pastor a perfect church, but I pastor a life-giving church. God is seeking congregations that give life. In his book *The Life-Giving Church,* Ted Haggard states, "I believe we need healthy, life-giving apostolic churches to disciple people, to raise up the next generation and to complete the Great Commission."[1] As I read Ted's book, tears welled up in my eyes, because this brother knows what he's talking about. When people come to your church, they ought to encounter Jesus. When we encounter him, we have church.

How to Lead With Pleasure

You may be thinking, "Well, put some handles on this pleasurable encounter with Jesus. What does it look like?" Here are some basic guidelines.

Worship him every day. Take time out of your pastoral day to worship God.

Pray, and shut up when you pray. Listen to God. What's he telling you about your church?

Preach Jesus. Preach Jesus, crucified and resurrected. Preach Jesus always. Never quit preaching Jesus.

Love people. Love people at their worst times as well as their best times. Don't be a selective people-lover, loving only when it's convenient or beneficial to you. Love as Jesus loves.

I'll never forget the words of Dr. Rollin S. Burhans, my childhood pastor. When he learned I was called to the ministry, he called me into his office and said, "I'm going to tell you something very important."

"Doc B, what is it?"

"Love God, and love the people."

In the past twenty years, I've read books, attended seminars, and networked. The greatest truth still holds. "Love God, and love the people." It is the key to a full life, to intimacy, and to understanding what it means to be a leader in God's church.

"Love God, and love the people."

I hope I've challenged you to crawl up into the lap of Jesus, get a hug, and be so full of God that you would love the world with such intensity that you can no longer tolerate it being trashed by an evil enemy. I hope you'll love so deeply that you will include everyone in your invitation to come and be nourished by Jesus. People who have fallen in love—*madly* in love, *crazy* in love—enjoy it. And they want others to enjoy it too.

Wedding Checklist

1. Be honest. Is your ministry a pleasure or a burden right now?

2. What has robbed your ministry of pleasure?

3. Describe a time in your life when you led from the heart. What were the factors that made that possible?

4. Write down all the possibilities that God has for you in your church. Imagine every person in your congregation intimately connected to Jesus Christ.

5. How can you begin to recapture the heart of your church and lead your congregation into joyful participation?

Vision:

Leading the Bride's Mind

Vision begins with mission. Vision exists because the mission isn't completed yet. Without mission, vision is vague. Without vision, the mission will not be accomplished. Vision and mission are directly linked. If you're going to lead the bride of Christ, part of your job is to awaken the church's mind to the possibilities of Jesus. That's vision!

Where's the Mission?

When I visit churches and listen to church leaders, I become increasingly aware of a problem that's emerged in the church: We're not convinced that it's our mission to connect people with Jesus. We've lost our connection to the Great Commission. The church is to go into the world (Matthew 28:18-20). We're to be *in* the world, yet not *of* the world. That's where Jesus is. But that's not where many churches are.

Pastors in America must choose between maintaining their churches and instilling a passionate vision in their churches. I continually remind our church that one of my greatest fears is that someday we will be satisfied with just being a church and will thus cease to be a mission. In fact, the only reason we are a church is that we're willing to engage in the mission.

The only reason we are a church is that we're willing to engage in the mission.

We must constantly remind our churches and ourselves of our mission and vision. Other people are always waiting to be connected to Christ. *Our work in the church is never done.* The mission isn't complete, which means we always require fresh vision.

Many pastors get distracted from their vision and mission. They marry themselves to systems, processes, and structures, and they lose their way. At Hillvue, we led our community of faith from a structured, organized meeting house to a place where people are on a mission to connect others to Jesus Christ. Now, instead of having *set* ministries, we have *evolving* ministries. Every day, something new begins to emerge that allows us to connect people to Jesus in more effective ways. If we'll point people to a connection with Jesus, instead of seeking only to staff our structures and programs, the church will grow.

We must be convinced of the mission of Jesus, and we must constantly remind our church through every means possible of that mission. Here are the truths we need to keep in the forefront of our minds:

- Jesus loves the church.
- It's Jesus' church, not our church.
- Jesus is the head of the church; we're not the head of the church.
- Jesus is responsible for saving people; we can't save them or change them. However, we are responsible for presenting Christ to people.
- All things are possible with Christ.
- The church is an everlasting entity; the things of the world are not. The methods, systems, and techniques employed by the church are temporary; they are not the triumphant weapons of the church.
- Ways and means constantly change. Jesus, however, does not. He stays in his mission to connect people to the kingdom of God and constantly and consistently changes their lives.

A Mission Attitude

Being convinced of the mission also leads us to adopt the attitudes of Jesus. When we're convinced, we get attitude. For the past twelve years, the attitude at Hillvue Heights Church has been "whatever it takes."

Churches, especially those of you who are one-hundred–member churches in rural areas, listen to this truth: You

Passion Point

What mission is guiding your vision? What vision is carrying out your mission?

must become convinced that you're supposed to connect people to Jesus Christ. Notice that I didn't specify how many people you need to connect. Numbers are irrelevant; people are totally relevant. Homes in your setting may be five miles apart. You may not have connected a thousand people to

Jesus this year, but your church must be convinced that its mission is to reach and connect your community to Christ. You need to expose and reveal Jesus to everybody in your area. I want you to hear this. Are you in a life-giving, God-honoring, convinced church and are you doing whatever it takes to get the gospel message out to the people? Do whatever it takes.

Do whatever it takes.

Where Hillvue's Vision Began

When I began my ministry at Hillvue, we had no money, no facilities, and no reputation of being a loving church. Then we became convinced that God had called us to be a loving church. We became convinced that God was able. We became convinced that only God could do it.

About six years later, we had built a new building, grown a little bit, and seen some success. We began to rest on what "had been." As soon as we did, new words began to enter our vocabulary. For example, I would hear a staff member say, "We can't do this if we don't have that." These were words that had been foreign to our church during the previous six years.

After God started blessing us, we started thinking we had something to do with it. In fact, our only role was to be convinced that God could do it. When we believe in him, *his* power flows through us.

Our staff had to enter a time of serious repentance. We realized that we had to do whatever it takes to fulfill our mission. It involved work, headaches, toil, time, and energy. It involved being involved. It involved my entire life and everything I am. But this level of involvement is not painful if we're convinced that our mission is to reveal Christ and connect others to him. If we're convinced the church is about us, everything we do will always be a great burden because it interrupts us.

I noticed that our planning began to be driven by our personal schedules instead of what was best for the church. In leadership, we have to be careful. It's not *our* ministry; it's *his* ministry. This means that we have to learn to reschedule events and ministry opportunities for the greater good of the community. We have to learn to say no to some ministry opportunities so that we can say yes to greater ones. Becoming convinced of the message *changes everything.*

When the mission of connecting people to Jesus becomes the church's vision, everybody's schedule changes for Jesus. He's always on call to connect with whoever needs the connection.

Preparing for Vision the Jesus Way

Before you begin the process of defining a vision for your church, you'll need to do some spiritual spadework. You must spend personal, serious, and intentional time with Jesus. You must go out on that date. Listen, and don't talk much. Let Jesus do all the talking. Listen so intently that you might change your direction. God will always speak truth to us. Our job is to listen.

The bride's vision must come from the Groom. The Groom tells the bride what he wants in the context of unhurried communion. Vision doesn't start in the boardroom. It starts in the prayer room. Be sure that you approach visioning in a spiritual and Christ-centered manner. There's really no other alternative for the bride seeking to do the will of her Groom.

———————————————————————————————————

Vision doesn't start in the boardroom. It starts in the prayer room.

———————————————————————————————————

Vision at Hillvue

I want to share Hillvue's vision with you, not because you should imitate it, but because we learn by seeing what others do. As you read about our vision for our community, I hope God will begin to reveal a vision to you for your community.

There are three components to the vision of Hillvue Heights Church that have also been translated into five other church starts.

The first component of our vision is this: *We're convinced that Jesus Christ wants to change people's lives.* In our tradition, we call this a conversion, which we define as that point when a person accepts and receives the power of Jesus' cross and resurrection and thereby obtains a changed life. In this way, people's natures are changed. They're transferred from a state of death to a state of life. They're new people who are being transformed into the likeness of Christ. God desires that all of us would be connected with him and have this experience. Our church considers connecting people to a life-changing experience with Jesus paramount.

Second, *we are convinced that Jesus heals people.* It's simple: Jesus helps us get our lives back together. Jesus heals the wounds in our lives, whether they are physical or emotional. Jesus Christ brings us to wholeness. We are better people when we let Jesus into our lives.

When people come to our church, they get better. No matter what kind of people they are or where they are, they get better. We can't really look at the quantity, process, or completion of their healing progress. We just pray and hope that every day in the life of the church, we all get better together.

Also, we've come to realize that everybody in the church is wounded in some way. We all need healing. Our church is not just for those who have had tremendous struggles in life; it's for all of us. We are convinced that Jesus will guide us through all of our struggles.

And we've realized that even our best efforts can't fix other people. Only Jesus can.

The third component of our vision deals with *the development of the believer and activation into ministry.* We believe everybody in the church is a player in the mission. Everybody gets to participate. Everybody gets face time. Everybody's got a purpose with God. Everybody has the ability to connect people to Jesus.

I think of my buddy Ronnie, who's the coffee man at our church. For almost ten years, he's risen early on Sunday mornings simply to make coffee. He makes coffee in such a way that he connects people to Jesus.

I think of my buddy Rodney, who has long hair. We call him Hippie. Hippie's up early every Sunday morning, before anybody else arrives, to prepare to park cars. He wants people to connect to Jesus, and he parks cars in such a way that they will want that connection. He is convinced that

Jesus is the way, the truth, and the life, and he's convinced that it is his mission to help others.

Both of these servants are passionate about everything they do, no matter what it is, because they know their actions reveal their mission to connect people to Jesus. We believe people will develop into ministers of grace.

These three elements have helped guide our church to connect people to Jesus. But first we had to become convinced that Jesus desires that people come to him and allow their lives to be changed, that he can heal and will help people get better, and that he desires all people to participate in his ministry. These three elements have birthed countless ministry events and creative ideas. They continue to emerge as the city is blessed by a group of people who have become convinced that Jesus has called them, loves them, and has placed them on a mission to bless others.

Convinced That Jesus Can Do It

No matter where you're located, these attitudes can change how your church affects its particular community. Be convinced, because the bottom line is that *God* is convinced you can do it.

When people become convinced of these three things, strange and wonderful things happen. Again and again, the New Testament describes the process of convincing. Think about Saul. Sure that everything Jesus had done was wrong, he *fought* the church. The process of convincing him otherwise culminated on the road to Damascus. Once Paul was convinced, the change became evident to everyone around him. This convinced, changed person wrote about a third of the New Testament.

Who are the Sauls who need to be turned into Pauls in your church? Maybe it's you. Maybe you're in a small church, and you're convinced that it can't do anything. If that's the case, your attitude will *keep* you in a small church and you *won't* do anything. God doesn't have small churches; he has a bride that can do great things. You need to become convinced that God can use you to do all things.

143

I am amazed at what God has done in some of the people at Hillvue, in people who weren't going to be involved. One man has a quadriplegic son. When he and his family moved to our city, he had given up on finding a church that they could connect with. In fact, he told his wife he was going to "chill out" from the church for a while. She saw a wheelchair ramp at Hillvue and knew it would be possible to get her son inside on Sundays. So she convinced Andy to give church one more try. They came to Hillvue, and he wasn't certain he liked it. After a few Sundays, he decided he did like it and became convinced that God wanted to use him. Now he's a deacon.

Passion Point

Dream God-sized dreams, pastor. Dream, church located in Nowhere Land. What would happen if a few more in your congregation became convinced that God could do impossible things with them?

I think of a buddy named Don who had been through a divorce and wasn't sure about this whole Jesus thing. He allowed Jesus to come into his life and became convinced that he was connected to God. He became convinced that Jesus had saved him. He became convinced that he has a message to share. On a recent Wednesday night, I walked by the class he was teaching, and it was packed with people wondering how he became convinced.

You Can Dream Again

Don't you love being with people who dream big dreams? Dreamers are exciting, and their attitudes are contagious.

I pastor a church full of people who aren't supposed to be in church or leading other people to a connection with Christ. And it all began with a dream. Let me show you how much God can change things when you dream.

Remember the story I told you earlier about a fifty-seven-year-old atheist who gave it up for Jesus on Easter Sunday, 2001? At the beginning of 2002, we had the following conversation.

"Hey, Preach."

"What?"

"Guess what I'm going to do."

"I don't know. What are you going to do?"

"I'm going to work in the nursery. I didn't used to like kids. But you know, since Jesus has come into my life, I like kids—and a *lot* of things I never used to like. I'm going to work with the kids."

Don't doubt who God is, because God will take those who didn't use to like kids and teach them how to be lovers of children. This is another metaphor for the church. We need to learn to love the children, the children of God, the children of this world. We need to constantly be aware that God accomplishes the impossible. When you're convinced of that, you will *live* in possibilities.

How do we start dreaming again? We begin with a simple statement: "Lord Jesus, I surrender my understanding to your understanding. I will trust you with the elements of life that I do not understand. Where I do not have answers, I'll trust that you are the answer. Where I do have an answer, I'll check to see if it's your answer and not mine. Lord, I'm convinced that you are *it*. Because of you, all things are held together. Because of you, anything can happen."

Passion Point

Are you confident in your relationship with Jesus? Are you confident that Jesus will do what he says he will do?

Visioning With Confidence

As a church becomes confident in Christ, Jesus is able to work fervently through the congregation. Confidence isn't cockiness or arrogance. It is the ability to believe, understand, and activate. If we're not confident

Passion Point

Think about your personal ministry. What are you confident in? Think about the business sessions in your church. Where do the people turn to find the motivating power to get the task done? Do they turn to money? to building structures? to the church's history? to its tradition? its bylaws? How many times do they turn to other sources before they turn to Jesus, not believing that Jesus Christ's ministry is greater than their own interpretation or cultural viewpoint? How many of them believe that Jesus will do what he said he would do?

that Jesus is our own, *personal* Lord or that he is doing a great work in *us*, we will have a difficult time dreaming, visioning, and activating our ministries.

Are we in the church convinced that Jesus Christ died on the cross, providing forgiveness and connection to the eternal God? We can be convinced of that theologically, but are we confident of that practically? Are we confident that God will change the people we connect with? Confidence in Jesus Christ leads to activated ministry. The more confident we are in Jesus, the more we'll dream about engaging the world.

If we're willing to trust Jesus and activate our faith through our confidence in him, we'll see supernatural results. We cannot use our minds alone to find our way through ministry. Now, I'm not saying we shouldn't think. There are times we must be logical and pragmatic. But we must also be confident that trusting Jesus will evoke the supernatural in our midst.

Pastors and leaders ask me all the time, "Ayers, why don't I see the works of Jesus Christ in my church?" One strong possibility is that they're not allowing room for the works of Christ. We must decide what and whom we're going to put our confidence in.

I get tickled when I get around pastors; some are so proud of their academic achievements. You must call them Dr. So-and-So or Reverend

So-and-So. Unfortunately, you'll never obtain confidence by your title. Confidence is gained by seeing that Jesus is at work and changing lives. That's what allows God to unleash the supernatural in our churches.

You'll never obtain confidence by your title. Confidence is gained by seeing that Jesus is at work and changing lives.

Confidence in Crisis

Jesus demonstrated in his earthly life where we should place our confidence. Have you noticed that Jesus was always confident in a crisis? When we as church leaders fall apart, Jesus sees an opportunity for ministry. Jesus takes our crises and turns them into an illustration of his power. John 6 provides a prime example of this. If you've ever been on a finance team, you will relate to this episode.

When we as church leaders fall apart, Jesus sees an opportunity for ministry.

Jesus called Philip to his side and said, "Philip, where shall we buy bread for these people to eat?"

Philip responded that there was no way they had enough money to buy enough food for all the people.

Philip knew he didn't have the capability to feed all the people. He was certainly convinced they had a problem, but he was not convinced that it had a solution. How many times we all do this! We know we need to reach our communities. We know we need to engage with people who aren't connected with Jesus Christ. We know theoretically that God can heal people, but we really don't want to take that next step, which is being confident that Christ will do it.

Jesus knew that he could solve the problem, but he wanted Philip to understand that only Jesus could do it. I've spent twelve years learning this

As we minister in the twenty-first century, we have to ask ourselves how confident we are that the Jesus who walked on the earth some two thousand years ago will still evoke ministries with supernatural power. I say, "Absolutely." Being confident in God's power leads us to God's provision and God's perspective. It enables us to preach the gospel unashamedly and boldly, without worrying about who it offends but considering who it might change and engage. If we do this, we'll grow. We'll multiply. We'll connect. We'll reproduce. Our faith will deepen.

Who are you confident in? When people enter your church, what do they know it believes in?

simple truth. Only Jesus can solve our problems.

Have you realized that you cannot change your church? Have you learned that your degree, knowledge, theology, and denominational affiliation really cannot move your church? If all of our activity led to fervent discipleship, George Barna wouldn't have anything to write about. How can he describe so much shallowness in the American church experience if we're really engaging confidently in Christ?

I remember going on dates in high school and thinking, "This girl is just too good-looking. She's not going to have anything to do with me. I'm just a country boy. I play football. I'm really not intelligent enough." I remember sitting in school with a test in front of me, and having absolutely no confidence. "There's no way I'm going to pass this test. I *know* I'm going to fail." Guess what happened? I failed the test.

Jesus says, "Go and win your community." But sometimes, when I look at our community, it looks too fortified and strong, and I feel hopeless. I must become confident of what God is doing in the community. Confidence evokes ministry. Confidence in the right things changes everything. Our hope is in Jesus Christ. Jesus takes the bread. He takes the fish. He blesses them and feeds the multitude. The people who met Jesus on the hill that day walked away changed because they had been fed.

Deathbed Confidence

One cold, winter night, I received a call from an old buddy who was scared because he thought he was about to die. He had seen the doctor about his heart. The doctor wasn't sure what was going on.

He had struggled with a connection with Jesus Christ for a long time, wondering if it was real. I walked into his dimly lit room, and I could tell he was depressed. He asked me one question. "Preacher, I want to know one thing. And I want a simple, short answer. I want to know how you know you're saved. How do you know, without a doubt, that Jesus is going to take you to heaven? What have you done to know you're going to heaven?"

Deep in my soul, I was in intense prayer. I knew I needed a Jesus answer. This man knew all the traditional answers of the church. I prayed, "Jesus, I need you to speak, because he doesn't need to hear from another preacher. He's heard from enough preachers."

I looked my buddy in the eye and said, "I am confident that what Jesus said is true, and Jesus said that, if I would trust him, he would forgive me. If I would believe he died and rose, if I invited him into my life, he would save me. I am confident that Jesus is not a liar. I believe I'm going to heaven because Jesus said so. That's the bottom line."

Confidence is learning to truly believe that what Jesus said is reality. What he says is true. And what this man learned on his deathbed, we need to learn in our leadership: Jesus can be trusted with our future. Jesus can be trusted to carry out your church's vision.

Vision That Rocks the Boat

I'm amazed at how focused we are on comfort and how many books have been written on making the world comfortable with Jesus. Jesus never worried too much about making us comfortable. I laugh when I think about the church's search for comfort. I think about those disciples and the uncomfortable positions they were in on their journey with Jesus.

I think about that episode described in Mark 4, where the disciples were out in the middle of the lake when a bad storm arose. The waves began to break over the boat. The disciples *knew* they were going to drown. Jesus didn't even wake up! The disciples' confidence lay in their ability to navigate and bail water. Jesus stood up and said, "Quiet. Be still." And he calmed the storm.

The disciples asked, "Who is this? Even the wind and the waves obey him." They learned from this intensely uncomfortable experience where they should have placed their confidence.

At Hillvue Heights Church, we believe we're on a mission to help people change their lives, to help people discover the healing nature of Jesus Christ, and to help all those who engage in the church develop into ministers of God's grace and carriers of the plan. Again and again, I have seen that, as people become *convinced* of the gospel, they need to become *confident* of the gospel.

Turning the Ship Around

People ask me, "How did this church turn around? How did it become renewed? What did you do?"

I answer simply, "For the first time in my life, I trusted Jesus with the church." Sometimes we gain confidence only when our lives are placed in impossible situations.

Sometimes we gain confidence only when our lives are placed in impossible situations.

If you look closely at the New Testament, you'll see that the way people illustrated their confidence in Jesus was to give their lives *fully* to impossible situations. This has certainly been true at Hillvue. Nothing at this church was supposed to work. On paper, it didn't work financially. Theoretically, it didn't line up with church methodology. Logistically, according to the experts, a church could never grow there. I had only one thing to hold on to. I believed Jesus had sent my wife and me to this location to begin a church and that Jesus would change people's lives.

I was not encouraged by other pastors to accept the pastorate of Hillvue Heights Church. In fact, those older colleagues who were committed to a system of church said I would ruin my career if I went there. But the first time I stood in the pulpit of that church I knew that this was where God had called us. People asked me how we were going to do church. I said, "We're going to put everything in the past behind us. We're going to allow Jesus to take hold of us. We're going to take this church heavenward in Christ Jesus."

Theologically I was convinced. However, it took several years to become confident. We had low offerings, poor buildings, an organ that sounded like a circus organ, and a choir that could rarely find the right pitch. Finally, though, we developed confidence that Jesus was going to change each one of us—and our city.

When we read about the wonderful ways God has blessed some churches, we forget that God wants to bless every church. If you're in one of those churches of one to two hundred members and you feel that God cannot do great things in your church, look at me as living proof that God can use you, no matter who you are. Take your church. Teach that church. Preach to that church. Love that church into confidence in Jesus Christ.

Jesus wants to bless the world. From the day he was born on earth to the day he ascended into heaven, he espoused one consistent theme: "I am here to bless the world." We need to grab hold of the concept of blessing the world, and we need to be confident that Jesus *will* bless the world.

Vision *in* (not *for*) the Building Program

Before I came to Hillvue in 1991, the people in the church were wounded by a building program that left a debt of $450,000, no pastor, and a small congregation of only thirty left to pay the tab.

Five years later, it was evident that Hillvue had to build a new worship center. We were conducting four services on Sundays, bringing more than a thousand people through a chapel that accommodated only 350 to 400 people.

However, I had a confidence problem. I knew Jesus had done marvelous things for five years, but when I thought of constructing a building, I thought, "Oh, no, here we go again. We've had a church where Jesus has really worked, and now a building program will ruin it."

One of the deacon elders saw the situation differently. In a meeting, he said, "We must build now. We're going to drop the ball. We're not going to be able to do our ministry without more space."

I said, "I'm not worried about the building."

"You can't keep preaching four services each Sunday forever. It's time for us to build."

You see, he was confident that Jesus could build a building. I was confident that Jesus could build a church, but I wasn't convinced that Jesus could handle a building program. I knew that if we put up a building, we were risking fights, dissension, discord, and everything else that would come with a building project.

Finally, the deacon challenged me by saying, "Pastor, do you have enough faith to believe that Jesus can build a building?" When he put it like that, I was stuck. I realized that, when it came to the building program, I had focused on the problems and had taken my eyes off the possibilities of Jesus. My experience showed me that building projects cause problems for most Baptist churches. I didn't want to have a church full of problems; I wanted to have a church full of the power of Jesus.

Finally, I said, "OK, if we've got to build a building, I can't build it. I don't want to build it. Even so, we've got to build a building." Through a long process of prayer and listening to Jesus, I became *confident* that Jesus could do it and *confident* that God had called people to get it done with excellence. You know what I found? Jesus already knew my fears and had already appointed people to build the building.

The deacon elders and I agreed that we would set aside thirty days for prayer to discover who should be on the building team. We didn't comb the congregation. We didn't send out surveys looking for the most qualified and experienced builders in the church. We *prayed* and asked God for seven names. (When I tell stories like this, some people say, "Oh, yeah, really." Really, these things happen when you place your confidence in Jesus.) God gave me seven names. I wrote them down, asked my secretary to sign the paper, sealed it in an envelope, and put it in my desk drawer.

At the next deacons meeting, each person presented a list, and we wrote the names on a dry-erase board. Every one of us had the same seven names. I began to be confident, because I knew that this was not coincidental. It was God saying, "These people can do it."

We trusted those people to do it. They built a worship center efficiently and with excellence. It is still used to fulfill the mission of the church. We built a worship center with absolutely no fights, because we listened to how Jesus wanted it to be done. *Everything* in the church has to be done by Jesus, even the smallest details.

We built a worship center with absolutely no fights, because we listened to how Jesus wanted it to be done.

Passion Point

Think about your ministry. Does it call people to commit? Does it call them to engage in the life of the church? Does it encourage them to become engaged with Jesus Christ? What are you calling the people in your church to be? Note the wording here. Not to do, *but to* be. *We've spent way too much energy calling people to do* things in the church.

We need to ask, "How do we do it, Jesus?" Jesus does it differently than we do it. His way is never offensive. It's never obnoxious. It's full of grace. It's always full of mercy. Know and be confident in the Spirit of Jesus. Know also that your confidence in Jesus engages the curiosity of the world. Be a Spirit-led visionary, and Jesus will accomplish through you more than you ever thought possible.

Wedding Checklist

1. Here's a practical idea for your next leadership meeting: Ask the leaders what they're confident in. Is it Jesus?

2. How could Jesus be included in your vision statement?

3. Want to throw it all on the line? Ask members of your staff to pray for thirty days about what Jesus wants to do through your church. Then call them together to learn what they heard.

    Warning: Be ready to hear Jesus speak.

4. Make a list of everything in your church that needs to be "turned around." Then begin to develop a vision of how Jesus might radically change those aspects of your church.

5. Here's the vision challenge of a lifetime: How would you summarize the vision of your church in one word? What is the operative term in your church's core vision?

Faithfulness:

Helping the Bride Endure

What has God ultimately called the bride to do? Simply to be faithful. Faithfulness is the constant challenge of the church. It's the constant challenge of church leadership. As a pastor, I am called to be *faithful* to Jesus Christ; to be faithful to my own personal relationship with him in grace; to be faithful in my leadership; to be a man of integrity; to teach, preach, and disciple; and to show people the way of Christ. I must do this through my own life as well as through teaching the Word of God correctly. To share grace, live grace, and be faithful to grace is the greatest challenge of my life.

Where have you placed your faith? The word *Jesus* may automatically pop into your mind, but look at your daily routine. Open that Palm Pilot, see that schedule, and discover who you're really faithful to. It's so easy to get caught up in the church's structure, organization, and pace. It's easy to forget that all of it is about Jesus. It's not about the congregation. It's not about leadership. It's about being faithful to Jesus. If we would always remember that it's about faithfulness, it would alleviate so much anxiety in the church.

It's not about leadership. It's about being faithful to Jesus.

It doesn't matter if you're in a congregation of five thousand or of fifty. The bold question still remains: Are you being faithful to Jesus Christ? Jesus isn't counting numbers. If you look closely into the Scriptures, especially the Gospel of Mark, you'll find that Jesus was never impressed with crowds. He's impressed with faithfulness.

For example, in the midst of the crowd, the confusion, and the chaos, Jesus' power slipped into a woman who was faithful enough to touch the hem of his garment. Jesus stopped, even amid a crowd and a pressing schedule to recognize someone who was faithful and said, "Your faith has healed you" (Mark 5:34).

The Unfaithful Bride

God is faithful to us, even when we're unfaithful to him. It's in that prophetic book of Hosea that God illustrates to us his longing love for a faithful bride. Hosea was commanded to marry the harlot Gomer, who was unfaithful before and after marriage. God directed Hosea to marry Gomer and to reclaim her. We have a God who reclaims us, even in the midst of our unfaithfulness.

We become more radiant and effective the more we understand that we're to be faithful to Jesus Christ. God is faithful to us. He sent Jesus Christ to die and to rise again. He asks us to be faithful to that message. God isn't impressed with pedigrees. Paul said, "I have it all. I come from the right family. I'm a Pharisee of Pharisees. I've been to the right schools. I understand the right things...I consider all of that rubbish compared to knowing Jesus Christ as my Lord and Savior." Then Paul went on to say, "I will join in the sufferings of Jesus to understand the power of his resurrection" (Philippians 3:5-11, paraphrased).

Where are you with Jesus? Are you struggling, worrying about being successful? We need to reframe the whole idea of success in ministry. We need to ask how we become a successful bride. How do we become effective pastors? By showing faithfulness in whatever situation God has placed us.

The Scripture says that those who are faithful with little can be given much. However, having much doesn't necessarily mean that we've been faithful. We can have things of this world and totally miss the things of Christ. Once again, who are you faithful to? Is it your denomination? Is it your family? Is it your congregation? Is it your image? Is it your understanding of the call? Is it your academic excellence? Is it your ability to phrase words to motivate people? Are you faithfully committed to the cause of Jesus to go—teaching, preaching, discipling, and telling others the good news of Christ?

We can have things of this world and totally miss the things of Christ.

Or are you faithful to sit at the feet of Jesus and simply bask in his love? As a leader, do you say, "Jesus, your way is greater than my way. I will follow you"?

King David showed us how easily once-faithful leaders can fall. He had such faith that he used a stone in a slingshot to slay a giant. But in a weak moment, at the height of his power, he looked across a rooftop and was seduced, forsaking faithfulness to God in a moment of temptation.

There's temptation in the ministry. Don't, for one minute, think that those ordination papers run the temptation away. Don't think for a moment that the title *pastor* scares the devil. Don't think for a moment that simply positioning yourself in the church automatically leads you to discovering the deeper truths of God. Faithfulness to Jesus in the midst of temptation—that's the struggle: to surrender to Jesus, even when the winds of temptation are blowing all around you.

Don't, for one minute, think that those ordination papers run the temptation away. Don't think for a moment that the title **pastor** *scares the devil.*

Never forget that there is a seducer. There is a devil. There is a struggle. There is a war. The devil wants to sabotage all of your attempts to be faithful.

In *Wild at Heart,* John Eldredge describes the battle with Satan: "Finally, he probes the perimeter, looking for a weakness. Here's how this works: Satan will throw a thought or a temptation at us in hopes that we will swallow it. He knows your story, knows what works with you and so the line is tailor-made to your situation."[1]

The devil despises faithful people. The eleventh chapter of Hebrews is not about ultimate achievement in the world's eyes; it's about holding to faith, even when the world thinks you're ridiculous. If there's one thing the world needs to see today, it's a ridiculous church—a church that loves people through all things, reflects the power of God regardless of the circumstances, stands in the truth of Jesus Christ in spite of a culture opposed to him, and does not bow down or forsake the glory of God's community for foolish practices that bring momentary glory.

Temptations That Steal Faithfulness

I want to talk about a few of the temptations that constantly surround us in leadership. Beware of them. Don't fall to them. Resist them. When they come your way, run away from them.

The first temptation is to use our own strength, power, and strategies to do what only God can do. God calls us to be faithful to his power. Let's constantly remember that our strength is limited and cannot create eternal possibilities. Jesus' strength is sufficient for all things.

As a young pastor, I spent hours each week counseling people. Guess what I discovered. None of them got better, because I was powerless to change their lives. What they needed was an honest encounter with Jesus Christ. What I was giving them, even with a good heart and good intentions, was my understanding. They needed *God's* power.

Our strength cannot change a human life. Beware. You'll constantly be tempted to use your power, your strategy, and your approach to drive the church. It's ironic that what some churches need is less money instead of more money. With less money, they would depend on *God's* power instead of material provisions to guide them. Sometimes what the church needs is a smaller building instead of a larger building. Then the people who attended would be impressed with the right thing instead of the church structure.

What some churches need is less money instead of more money. With less money, they would depend on **God's** *power instead of material provisions to guide them.*

God isn't impressed with our buildings, power, strength, and intellect. God is seeking our faithfulness. Through faithfulness, we begin to move in the power of God. The good news is that when humanity exhausts its possibilities, God creates more. Many times I've heard someone return from a visit to the hospital and say, "The doctors can do nothing now. I guess we ought to pray." Maybe we ought to be praying all the time, not just when the doctors run out of possibilities. We'll always be tempted to use our own strength, our power, instead of God's.

Human beings can create. There's no doubt about it. The only problem is that we cannot create anything that lasts forever. That includes church structures. Our methodologies change constantly because we are unable to create eternity. It's amazing that the grace of God has never changed. The way to God is still the same: the Cross and the Resurrection. The message has been through a plethora of cultural changes, but its power is undiminished. It was created and given by God's strength and power, not ours. May God's power move through you. When you're tempted to operate under your own power, surrender again and again and again to the strength of God. Even when God doesn't react as fast as we want him to, may the power of God come—in the power of God's timing.

The second temptation is the temptation to be recognized. Do they know who I am? Do they know what I've done? Do they know what I've achieved? Success. Success. Success.

My desk is littered with brochures telling me how to be a successful minister and how to run a successful church. What is a successful church? One that has gathered a crowd? I always laugh when I hear people say, "We had a great meeting. We had a lot of people there."

I say, "You didn't have as many as Van Halen did. They must be successful ministers; they draw *huge* crowds."

I always laugh when I hear people say, "We had a great meeting. We had a lot of people there."

I say, "You didn't have as many as Van Halen did. They must be successful ministers; they draw **huge** *crowds."*

Why don't we listen to the Scripture? Second Timothy says multitudes will be drawn to doctrine that tells them only what they want to hear. Jesus drew large crowds, but they thinned when he invited them to deny themselves, pick up a cross, and follow him. At this invitation, many left. Was he a failure? Hardly!

Who and what are recognized in your church? Is it the church's structure? Is it your denomination? Is it your organization? Is it the atmosphere? Is it the pastor's personality? Is it the music? Or, when people come to your church, do they recognize that Jesus resides there?

We'll always be tempted to seek recognition. We need to remember that we've already been recognized. Jesus knows us. Jesus has called us. Jesus loves us. "Blessed are the meek" (Matthew 5:5a). Do your ministry. Do the work. Pastors who are being faithful in smaller congregations are as large in God's eyes as any "big-time pastor." It's not about the size of the congregation; it's about faithfulness to the Lord. It's about allowing the glory of God, not human achievement, to be realized.

Oh, what a joy it is when our colleagues tell us, "You've done such a wonderful job." The truth is that it is Jesus who's done a wonderful job. Don't you dare take his credit!

The third temptation is to gain riches, position, power, and the wealth of the world. What a temptation! Satan offered Jesus the riches of the world (Luke 4:5-7). Satan has told many a pastor, "I'll give you the riches of the world if you'll just stay out of the Jesus business." I don't think the devil ever minds us going to an organization. The devil couldn't care less if we are a part of an institution. But the devil can't stand it when we position ourselves intimately with Jesus Christ.

A child of God, fully walking in the potential, power, and revelation of Jesus, is the devil's enemy. Organized "worship junkies" are not much of a threat to an evil entity, for they seek only a fleeting moment of personal satisfaction with the Deity who created them. Those who walk faithfully in the power and riches of God seek Jesus' way in every situation.

Be careful not to trade the riches of heaven for the wealth of the world. How many pastors have changed congregations over the issue of money alone, only to find themselves in out-of-context ministries?

Pastors rarely feel called to lower salaries. But sometimes God does call us to lower salaries. (I know this from personal experience!) Sometimes God calls us to see what we will give up so he might illustrate his power through us. Are we willing to go where God asks us to go? Those in the Bible who followed God usually had to give up their positions in life to do so.

"Drop your nets and follow me" (Matthew 4:18-20, paraphrased).

"Abraham, leave the land of your home and follow me" (Genesis 12:1, paraphrased).

"Moses, leave your position as a shepherd in the desert to be a deliverer and a revolutionary for my people in Egypt" (Exodus 3, paraphrased).

Beware! God calls us to give it up in order to get it on. When we succumb to the temptation of wealth, we rely increasingly on our system of power instead of God's system of power.

Those in the Bible who followed God usually had to give up their positions in life to do so.

Now, here's the lethal part: Power, recognition, and wealth all work together. They're fellows, chaps, mates. And they all have one purpose: to bring you down—along with the bride of Christ. If you want to make the bride a tramp, go ahead and flirt with these evils. Worse yet, give in to them.

This leads us to the fourth temptation, which is to be someone other than ourselves. Don't imitate some pastor out there whom you deem successful; let God make you who you are. The world's looking for authentic people, not imitations.

The professor of my undergraduate theater-appreciation class, Bill Leonard, gave me a nugget of truth that has stayed with me. He said that, at best, an imitation can only be second-best. Be very careful, church leader, not to imitate another leader, but to be in an intimate relationship with

Jesus Christ and allow the truth of God to shape your character, approach, design, and *your* execution of the ministry.

We pastors do such hilarious things. As Rick Warren was gaining prominence in the Christian community, many young pastors in Kentucky started wearing flowered shirts like those that are typically worn in California. Flowered shirts just don't go well in *Kentucky*. Be who you are. If you're a suit-and-tie pastor, be a suit-and-tie pastor. If you're a blue-jeans-and-boots pastor, be a blue-jeans-and-boots pastor.

When you're expending energy imitating someone, you can forget to be like Christ. God calls us to be faithful to his image and his relationship, not to another person's approach. This doesn't mean we can't learn from each other; it means we need to present ourselves as God has created us. God has called *many* different types of people into the ministry, and no one type is more important than the others.

God honors authentic faith. When Jesus watched people making their offerings to God, he was not impressed with the rich and the wealthy. It was an impoverished *widow,* the least likely to be recognized, who impressed Jesus when she dropped her two small copper coins into the box. She was being authentically faithful to her God. Do likewise. Be who you are.

I must confess that being around preachers is sometimes the toughest thing I do. I've played on sports teams; I've worked in corporate America in many different organizations, on farms, and with construction crews. The group that has disappointed me the most because of its jealousy and pride is pastors. Be satisfied with who God has made you.

Authenticity works well in the twenty-first century. It's worked in all centuries. Be the person God called you to be, without apology. But let me warn you: Some people will really like you, and others really won't. Never forget that Jesus had the same experience. So don't apologize for who you are. Long to be recognized by Christ. Long to be authentic with Christ. Imitate, assimilate, and process the power of God in your own life so that the genuine person God has created will emerge.

As pastors, we put in many hours caring for people. We celebrate glory with them, and we help them endure agony. But over time we can become mechanical as we process the truth of God for our congregations, give instructions and declarations, provide care, and invite others to know Christ. Sometimes in the business of celebrating everybody else's connection with God, we forget to have one ourselves.

I was reminded of this pitfall one day by one of our young pastors who had been in ministry for only a month and a half. He asked, "When do you find time in this ministry to personally encounter Jesus?"

I said, "You must make the time and realize that it's as important as anything else you attempt."

After only six weeks of ministry, this young pastor had realized how easy it is to get so caught up in a ministry system that you stop developing your own relationship with Jesus. When we lose our intimate connection with Jesus, loneliness defines our lives in leadership. Joseph Stowell wrote, "The Prodigal's problem was that he thought his material and social world was sufficient. Self-sufficiency is life's greatest barricade to intimacy with God."[2] When loneliness enters our lives, the temptation to find intimacy, even false intimacy, becomes intensely real.

This leads to the fifth temptation: sexual temptation. To recover sensation, to find some kind of love, even a false love, can seem fulfilling when we're lonely.

Long before a minister enters into sexual sin, that minister has toyed with the other temptations. When we're tempted to use our own power, we're not using Christ's power, and we lose our resistance to temptation. When we're tempted to be recognized, it's hard for us to be connected. When we sell ourselves for wealth, we become empty, because wealth can never give us what only Jesus has. When we imitate other people, we become even more vulnerable and start to look for stimulation. It's Christ Jesus who must stimulate us to a full and abundant life; we can't do it by ourselves. It's pathetically easy for us to turn to our sexual nature to replace the sensation and depth of intimacy that only God can give.

It's pathetically easy for us to turn to our sexual nature to replace the sensation and depth of intimacy that only God can give.

The struggle of the church leader is always a struggle between love and lust. Will we prize Christ Jesus as our all in all, or will we value things of our own creation? Will we love the fleeting so much that we forsake the eternal?

Please don't stand in judgment of those pastors who have fallen into sexual sin. It's easier than any of us know. Actually, in a real way, we all know. Several pastors have sat in my office, brokenhearted and in tears. They were men of strong character and courage who faithfully spread the gospel, but they were lured slowly and seductively by their own power and celebrity. This led to loneliness and a desire to restore some feeling or sensation, which eventually opened the door to infidelity.

Sexual temptation surrounds us, and we need to be conscious of it. We live in a seductive, sensual world. We live in a world that says, "Do it now." We live in a world that says, "It doesn't matter; live for the moment." Jesus, however, calls us to live forever. True intimacy is in Christ. As you find intimacy with Christ, you'll find the ability to resist the allurement of sexual temptation.

I've been pastoring for twenty years—preaching, serving on church staffs, and listening to people. I've never encountered an incidence of infidelity that was positive or a blessing to anyone. The momentary pleasure always turned into a lifelong tragedy.

We're not for sale. Remember this the next time a prominent church member wants to give you a special donation so you might bend the Scripture just a little to justify his life. You're not for sale!

In 1993, one of our deacons was disgruntled because we were beginning to become a praise and worship church. He didn't appreciate that direction, nor did he feel it was of God. He claimed to have provided some of the church's financial resources, and he therefore felt he was entitled to say to me, "I want you to stop the church from continuing in this direction.

If you don't, my family and I are leaving, and I will pull my financial support from this church. It will not survive."

I answered him, "I hope you find a church that pleases you and fits your needs. May God's blessing go with you."

He was shocked. He left the church, and the next week the offering increased. I learned a valuable lesson: When you stand with Christ, he'll stand with you. If you sell out the first time, it's easier to sell out the second time. Before too long, you've completely sold out.

Dr. Joel Gregory, in his book *Too Great a Temptation,* illustrates how easy it is to become something you don't want to be. He spent some time with Dr. W.A. Criswell, who always drank whole milk over ice with his meals. Because Gregory was with Criswell, the kitchen staff began to serve milk with his meals as well. Gregory didn't dislike milk but wasn't used to drinking it with meals. To be polite, he drank the milk, and eventually he was cornered. If he told the kitchen staff he didn't want the milk, it would reflect on what they had done for weeks and embarrass them. Gregory wrote, "It was one of those situations where the longer it went, the more difficult it would be to call it off. So I drank milk."[3] You see, when you sell out on simple, little things that aren't you, you can end up in a bed you don't want to be in.

When you sell out on simple, little things that aren't you, you can end up in a bed you don't want to be in.

Be careful. We're a bride, not a harlot. There's not a "for sale" sign on the church. No amount of money, silver, gold, or platinum is worth the authenticity of your ministry. Don't forsake your ministry. Don't forsake your authentic identity in Christ.

We're a bride, not a harlot.

How to Remain a Faithful Pastor

The way to avoid lapsing into unfaithfulness is to stay faithful in the little things. Be faithful to the preaching of the gospel. As a pastor, learn to please Jesus, and don't evaluate yourself on the basis of acclaim. Learn to love people. Part of loving them is telling them the truth. Even in a culture that wants to indulge in harmful behavior, continue to tell the people that the behavior is harmful.

Remain faithful. You're in love with Jesus. And I have even better news. He's in love with you. Become a lover of God, and allow God to love you. This will help you resist other lovers who want to take the place of the greatest Lover of all.

I recently asked a pastor friend who had just retired, "In forty-two years of ministry, what's the word? If you had to sum it all up, what's the word?"

"Ayers, if you've got to make an error, always err on the side of grace. Number two, I hate to tell you this, but I think you could be right. There were times in my ministry when I loved the institution and denominational structure more than I loved Christ. Stay in love with Jesus."

A minister can feed hungry people, clothe naked people, captivate people with rhetoric, draw a crowd, motivate, have the ability to run a complicated organization, be acclaimed, and climb to the top. The tragedy is that this same pastor can miss an intimate relationship with Jesus Christ.

The Holy Spirit must drive the church. As we create the systems and structure, the cogs and machinery, to operate the organization of the church, it's easy to mistake the energy of our own organization for the movement of God. God lasts forever. We last for a moment. Listen. Speak softly. Move slowly. The wind of the Holy Spirit is always blowing and has been since the day of Pentecost. The closer you get to Jesus, the more you'll feel that wind. You'll know the right direction. You'll be willing to pay the price. You'll be faithful to the Groom.

Wedding Checklist

1. As a pastor, how do you define success?

2. Is faithfulness a cop-out for ineffective ministry? How are faithfulness and effectiveness balanced?

3. How do you evaluate your own success—on the basis of results or on the basis of faithfulness?

4. Is faithfulness a part of your job description? Is it a part of your staff's job descriptions?

5. How can your church encourage faithfulness?

Postscript
A Bride's Blessing

Bride of Jesus, may his glory pour into you. May his power move through you. May Jesus be recognized in you. May the riches of heaven come through you. May you be authentic in your position with Jesus. May the intimacy and love of Christ satisfy you. May the footsteps of Jesus outweigh the blueprint of your own plans. May the bride of Christ be realized forever and ever. May her radiance touch the world and illustrate to the world that Jesus loves us all and seeks to bring us faithfully to him as his bride. May Jesus hold you, walk with you, and love you. Until the bride is brought forth, forever, may we faithfully respond to the Groom.

Endnotes

Chapter Two

1. George Barna, *The Second Coming of the Church* (Nashville: Word Publishing, 1998), 2-8.
2. Steve Sjogren, *Conspiracy of Kindness* (Ann Arbor: Servant Publications, 1993), 24-31.
3. Ray Anderson, *The Soul of Ministry* (Louisville: Westminster John Knox Press, 1997), 82.

Chapter Three

1. Rory Bourke, Glen Ballard, and Kerry Chater, *You Look So Good in Love,* recorded by George Strait (Warner Chappell Music/MCA Music/Polygram Music Publishing, 1983).
2. Henri Nouwen, *Can You Drink the Cup?* (Notre Dame, IN: Ave Maria Press, 1996), 107.

Chapter Four

1. George Barna, *The Second Coming of the Church* (Nashville: Word Publishing, 1998), 23.

Chapter Six

1. Henri Nouwen, *Can You Drink the Cup?* (Notre Dame, IN: Ave Maria Press, 1996), 96.

Chapter Seven

1. Ted Haggard, *The Life-Giving Church* (Ventura, CA: Regal Books, 2001), 37-28.

Chapter Nine

1. John Eldredge, *Wild at Heart* (Nashville: Thomas Nelson Publishers, 2001), 163.
2. Joseph M. Stowell, *Far From Home* (Chicago: Moody Press, 1998), 49.
3. Dr. Joel Gregory, *Too Great a Temptation* (Fort Worth: The Summit Group, 1994), 270.

Group Publishing, Inc.
Attention: Product Development
P.O. Box 481
Loveland, CO 80539
Fax: (970) 679-4370

Evaluation for
Igniting Passion in Your Church

Please help Group Publishing, Inc., continue to provide innovative and useful resources for ministry. Please take a moment to fill out this evaluation and mail or fax it to us. Thanks!

● ● ●

1. As a whole, this book has been (circle one)

not very helpful   very helpful

| 1 | 2 | 3 | 4 | 5 | 6 | 7 | 8 | 9 | 10 |

2. The best things about this book:

3. Ways this book could be improved:

4. Things I will change because of this book:

5. Other books I'd like to see Group publish in the future:

6. Would you be interested in field-testing future Group products and giving us your feedback? If so, please fill in the information below:

Name_____

Church Name _____

Denomination _____ Church Size _____

Church Address _____

City _____ State _____ ZIP _____

Church Phone _____

E-mail _____

Exciting Resources for Pastors and Church Leaders

CounterCultural Christians:
Exploring a Christian Worldview With Charles Colson

Participants will gain deep insights in a fun-to-learn format with this interactive media kit. Video and audio presentations from Charles Colson set the stage for each session's dynamic group interaction. Grasp the underlying belief systems that impact how people view the world around them! Then dig into Scripture to guide your conclusions. This study will help group members learn how to develop a Christian worldview and transform culture.

Includes:
+ Video with twelve 3- to 5-minute segments featuring Charles Colson
+ CD with 12 *BreakPoint* audio segments
+ Leader Guide with tips and background information for each session
+ 6 Participant Guides with relational questions and activities

Charles Colson is a popular author, speaker, and radio commentator on the nationally syndicated *BreakPoint* broadcast (www.BreakPoint.org). He is author of *How Now Shall We Live?* and is a former presidential aide to Richard Nixon. Colson is founder of The Wilberforce Forum and founder of Prison Fellowship Ministries. In 1993, Colson was awarded the prestigious *Templeton Prize for Progress in Religion,* given for extraordinary leadership and originality in advancing humanity's understanding of God.

Tracey D. Lawrence is a freelance writer and founder of *Scribe Ink.* She holds a B.S. in Christian Education, a M.A. in Church History and Theology and is pursuing a D. Phil. Tracey has worked with such ministries as The Wilberforce Forum, Promise Keepers, Christian History Institute, and Focus on the Family.

ISBN 0-7644-2520-X $99.99

Additional Participant Guide
ISBN 0-7644-2522-6 $7.99

Flagship church resources
from Group Publishing

LeadingIdeas:
To-the-Point Training for Christian Leaders
Alan Nelson

Tangible, high-quality training on vital topics will guide leaders to be their best. Each 30-minute, easy-to-prepare lesson offers dynamic activities and in-depth discussions to help leadership teams grow. Topics include learning to spot potential leaders, determining how much to oversee, and modeling servant leadership. Perfect for leadership training courses, staff meetings—anytime leaders gather. Includes reproducible handouts.

ISBN 0-7644-2448-3 $17.99

Alan Nelson is the founding/lead pastor of Scottsdale Family Church. He has an MA in psychology/communications and a doctorate in leadership. Nelson writes a leadership/staff column for *Rev. Magazine* and for John Maxwell's e-zine, *Leadership Wired*. Nelson is a speaker/trainer for groups such as Willow Creek Association, Group Publishing, and the Billy Graham Evangelistic Association.

Morph!
The Texture of Leadership for Tomorrow's Church
Ron Martoia

Both visionary and practitioner, Martoia equips pastors to *morph*—and effectively minister in today's society. Keep church relevant and dynamic. Explore new ideas in leading the church of tomorrow. Challenge your thinking about how to "do" church, move beyond the status quo and see your church and ministry grow. *Morph!* is a leader-building resource perfect for church ministry staff to read and discuss together. Includes real-life examples from churches that are morphing to accomplish their God-given mission!

Ron Martoia has served as Lead Pastor and Transformational Architect at Westwinds Church in Jackson, Michigan, a church he planted 14 years ago. Martoia attended Trinity Evangelical Divinity School and earned a doctorate at Fuller Theological Seminary.

ISBN 0-7644-2450-5 $19.99

Discover our full line of pastoral, adult, youth and children's ministry resources at your local Christian bookstore, or write: Group Publishing, P.O. Box 485, Loveland, CO 80539. www.grouppublishing.com

Flagship church resources
from Group Publishing